Designing Effective Online Instruction

A Handbook for Web-Based Courses

Franklin R. Koontz
Hongqin Li
Daniel P. Compora

Rowman & Littlefield Education
Lanham, Maryland • Toronto • Oxford
2006

Published in the United States of America
by Rowman & Littlefield Education
A Division of Rowman & Littlefield Publishers, Inc.
A wholly owned subsidary of
The Rowman & Littlefield Publishing Group, Inc.
4501 Forbes Boulevard, Suite 200, Lanham, Maryland 20706
www.rowmaneducation.com

PO Box 317
Oxford
OX2 9RU, UK

British Library Cataloguing in Publication Information Available

Library of Congress Cataloging-in-Publication Data

Koontz, Franklin R., 1939–
  Designing effective online instruction : a handbook for web-based courses /
Franklin R. Koontz, Hongqin Li, Daniel P. Compora.
      p. cm.
  Includes bibliographical references.
  ISBN-13: 978-1-57886-386-0 (hardcover : alk. paper)
  ISBN-13: 978-1-57886-387-7 (pbk. : alk. paper)
  ISBN-10: 1-57886-386-4 (hardcover : alk. paper)
  ISBN-10: 1-57886-387-2 (pbk. : alk. paper)
  1. Web-based instruction—Design. I. Li, Hongqin, 1966– II. Compora, Daniel
P., 1965– III. Title.
  LB1044.87.K66 2006
  371.33'44678—dc22

                                                              2005031196

⊚™ The paper used in this publication meets the minimum requirements of
American National Standard for Information Sciences—Permanence of Paper
for Printed Library Materials, ANSI/NISO Z39.48-1992.
Manufactured in the United States of America.

Contents

Preface

INTRODUCTION

The designing of online courses requires a radical change in thinking in the way the instruction is designed and presented to the student. Going from the traditional classroom instructional environment to online instruction is like going from an instructional television lesson that transports students from the classroom to a distant country to be immersed in the history, culture, customs, and music to a silent movie where students may feel lonely, isolated, and ultimately responsible for their own learning. The designed instruction must create a learning environment that will accommodate students in this new online learning setting. The primary responsibility of the instructional designer is to make sure the online program accomplishes the learning goals, in other words, that the students learn what they are supposed to learn.

Courses taught in instructional design (ID) in the area of instructional technology are found in the majority of colleges of education. In some institutions instructional design is a required area of study. These courses introduce a myriad of traditional instructional design models suitable for traditional classroom instruction but not for the design of online instruction. To date, however, few, if any, research-based models using a systems approach are available to design Web-based instruction.

NEED FOR WEB-BASED ID MODELS

Traditional classroom design models are presently being taught and used for this new form of online instruction. Some designers and online instructors still contend that Gagné's nine events of instruction (1985) and Keller's (1983) ARCS model are sufficient to use when designing online instruction. These models address instructional strategies and motivational strategies. However, according to a recent study conducted by Dr. Xiangqin Sun in 2001, half of the 133 instructional designers who were surveyed indicated there was a need for a specific instructional design model to be created and used for Web-based courses. A second study conducted by Dr. Hongqin Li in 2003 using a Delphi technique also found the need for a specific instructional design model that addresses the unique nature of this type of instruction. The majority of the respondents to the survey indicated that the traditional models being used did not address the teaching/learning variables of Web-based instruction and that there was a need for a specific instructional design model dedicated to the design of online instruction. In addition, there was a call by teaching faculty and professional instructional designers for a specific model dedicated to designing Web-based courses.

A variety of online courses, degree programs, and certificate programs lack proper instructional design structure and are no more than cut-and-paste lecture notes or textbooks on a Web site. Many teaching faculty are still designing their courses on a trial-and-error basis using the same teaching and design techniques used for conventional classroom instruction and have no evidence of the effectiveness of their Web-based courses.

PURPOSE OF THE ASSIST-ME MODEL

The purpose of the ASSIST-Me model is to introduce an instructional design approach for Web-based instruction that may be used by teaching faculty who design instruction for online courses, professional instructional designers, and faculty who teach instructional design courses. The ASSIST-Me model, based on the Delphi research study *Investigation of an Instructional Design Model for Web-Based Instruction (WBI)* (Li, 2003), offers an instructional design procedure intended specifically for the unique nature of online courses. Design procedures were obtained from a panel of professional instructional designers and synthesized into a model that contains the essential steps to be included in the design process. The ASSIST-Me model describes a step-by-step procedure that demonstrates how online instruction may be designed.

The ASSIST-Me model for WBI is presented as an open-systems approach, in other words, once the analysis phase has been completed, the designer may begin to design other parts of the instruction and will not be forced to follow a lockstep linear system. The model gives the designer maximum flexibility when creating effective instruction.

The text will not explain, however, the user interface design, or how to put courses online. That instructional material is already available. The text will also not explain the production procedures of various media such as audio, video, multimedia development, and so forth. That instructional material is also available.

ORGANIZATION OF THE TEXTBOOK

This textbook is divided into two major parts. Part 1 deals with necessary background information about the concept of instructional design. Chapter 1 addresses the basics of instructional design procedures, the need for a new model and approach, some building blocks that will foster a better understanding of need for a design model for online courses, and basic characteristics of instructional design. Chapter 2 discusses what a well-designed lesson should include in the way of elements of learning, and various learning theories. This chapter deals with how our students learn and how we can design instruction that will enhance their learning. Chapter 3 discusses what the research says about online learning and what we know enables students to learn.

Part 2 of this text introduces the ASSIST-Me model and has its own introduction.

Chapter Organization

Each chapter begins with an outline of the chapter, knowledge objectives that should be considered, and a lexicon that introduces new vocabulary terms used in the chapter. At the end of each chapter, online case studies have been included to give you examples of how other online instructors have designed their courses.

ACKNOWLEDGMENTS

The authors would like to thank the faculty who participated in the online case studies and shared their online course designs. If you would like to learn more about their courses, you may e-mail them for additional information.

Dr. John Cryan, professor of early childhood, for sharing his undergraduate course "Philosophy and Practice in Early Childhood Education" in the Department of Early Childhood, College of Education, The University of Toledo. E-mail: john.cryan@utoledo.edu.

Dr. Earnest DuBrul, associate professor of biology, for his graduate course "Scientific Thought and Communication" in the Department of Biology, College of Arts and Science, The University of Toledo. E-mail: earnest.dubrul@utoledo.edu.

Dr. Ella Fridman, associate professor, engineering technology, for her undergraduate course "Applied Thermodynamics" in the Department of Engineering Technology, College of Engineering, The University of Toledo. E-mail: ella.fridman@utoledo.edu.

REFERENCES

Gagné, R. (1985). *The conditions of learning and theory of instruction*. (4th ed.). New York: Holt, Rinehart and Winston.

Keller, J. M. (1983). Motivational design of instruction. In C. M. Reigeluth (Ed.) *Instructional design theories and models* (pp. 383–434). Hillsdale, N.J.: Erlbaum.

Li, H. (2003). Investigation of a new instructional design model for Web-based instruction (WBI): A Delphi study. Unpublished doctoral dissertation, The University of Toledo, Toledo, OH.

Part 1

THEORY AND RESEARCH

CHAPTER 1

Online Instructional Design: What Is It?

CHAPTER OUTLINE

Why Is There a Need for a New ID Model?
The Need for Building Blocks! Back to Basics
   Communication
   Instruction
   Teaching
   Learning
   Instructional Design
   E-instructional Design
ID Model Basics—The ADDIE Model
Basic Characteristics of Instructional Design
   Student-Centered
   Oriented Toward Knowledge Objectives
   Practical Performance
   Directed Toward Observable and Measurable Student Outcomes
Distance Education, Distance Learning, or E-learning?
Web-Based Instruction
Summary
References

KNOWLEDGE OBJECTIVES

At the end of this chapter, you should be able to:

1. Explain why classroom instructional design (ID) models are used for WBI.
2. Explain the necessity to use an ID model specifically designed for WBI.
3. Describe the focal point of ID found in Schramm's communication model.
4. Define the importance of obtaining feedback from students.
5. Contrast the difference between instruction and teaching.
6. Define the key elements found in the process of learning.
7. Describe the key concepts found in ID.
8. Justify the ADDIE model as the basis of all ID models.
9. Define the basic characteristics of ID.
10. Compare and contrast distance learning and distance education.

LEXICON

Terms to know:

analysis stage	channel
asynchronous	communication

(continued)

(continued)

design stage	maximizing learning
development stage	noise
distance education	receiver
distance learning	sender
effect	SKA
evaluation stage	synchronous
feedback	synergetic effect
field of experience	system
implementation stage	teaching
instruction	transaction
instructional design (ID)	Web-based instruction (WBI)
learning	

"The mind, once expanded to the dimensions of larger ideas, never returns to its original size."

—Oliver Wendell Holmes

Let's take a fun quiz. Choose the *best* answer from the multiple-choice question:

What would happen if you fermented new wine in an old wineskin?

A. The new wine would take on the flavor of the old wineskin.
B. Old wineskins cannot be found.
C. The wine would not totally ferment.
D. The new wine would burst the old wineskin.

What was your answer?

If you selected A, *The new wine would take on the flavor of the old wineskin*, you are correct, but it is not the best answer. The old wineskin would flavor or taint the new wine. If a different flavor of wine was being fermented, the old wineskin would prevent the new flavor from developing due to the residue remaining in the old wineskin. And life is too short to drink bad wine.

If you selected B, *Old wineskins cannot be found*, you are again correct, but again, B is not the best answer. Traditionally, when wine was emptied from the original wineskin, it was discarded and not used again. It had served its purpose in fermenting new wine and the old wineskin was basically worn out.

If you selected C, *The wine would not totally ferment*, you are again correct, but it is still not the best answer. True, new wine could be poured into the old wineskin, but it would not totally ferment because the wineskin had already been used in the fermentation process and was probably very shabby at this point.

Well now, the only remaining answer for you to select is D, *The new wine would burst the old wineskin.* During the fermentation process, certain gases are released expanding the wineskin to its absolute limit. If the old wineskin were to be used for a second time, the wineskin could no longer be stretched and would burst. Besides, who wants to lose all of that new and good wine?

Metaphors are a great way to teach, and we can use a figure of speech or a phrase that designates one concept and apply it to another. The metaphor of pouring new wine into a new wineskin is illustrative of what is needed in Web-based instruction (WBI). Traditionally, we have used general classroom-based instructional design (ID) models to design new WBI. Essentially, this is the same as pouring new wine into old wineskins. The same and sometimes worn-out instructional strategies are still being used for a new type of instruction that we call *Web-based instruction*. The new instruction for Web-based courses must be placed into a new design model that can meet the new instructional needs of our students.

WHY IS THERE A NEED FOR A NEW ID MODEL?

Why do we need to know anything about new ID procedures? After all, some of us might have taught traditional classroom classes for years as well as online courses, and our students appear to be learning. Results from test scores show that our students are learning and, for the most part, receiving fairly good grades. Why can't we continue to create our WBI as we always have done? How difficult and time consuming will it be to use a model? If we use an instructional model, do we have to go through every step?

These and additional questions may be asked when a new approach has been suggested to design something we think we have already successfully done. According to the recent literature addressing the issue of student learning, the majority of designers frequently do not attempt evaluation of instruction during the time the instruction is being designed and very little or no evaluation of the effects of the instruction after the course has been completed (Moore & Kearsley, 1996). This lack of evaluation may not be completed for several reasons. It takes time to establish evaluation criteria and the evaluation instrument. It takes time to administer the instrument to the students and interpret the results. If what we find is negative and a redesign of instruction must be conducted, additional time must be committed to design a process. Time is very precious to all designers and teaching faculty. That being the case, how do we really know if our instruction is effective? Are the students learning what they are supposed to learn? How effective is our designed instruction? Do the students have difficulty understanding our instruction and course assignments? Can the students maximize their learning in a minimum amount of time?

Almost any model may be used to systematically design classroom instruction. It appears, however, that traditional classroom instructional models may not meet the needs or answer many of the problems that arise in the design of online courses (Li, 2003; Sun, 2001). Li (2003) found in her Delphi study that nearly 70% of the professional panel members agreed that a specific instructional model needs to be designed and used for Web-based courses. Traditional classroom ID models are not designed for the unique nature of distance learning; that is, the teacher is geographically separated from the student, and the student, for the most part, interacts independently with the instruction with delayed feedback. In addition, it is also readily accepted by experienced designers that an ID model is more of a *guide* for the design process. Again, Li found that nearly 68% of the panel members did not use all of the steps of the selected model. The designer may use his or her own judgment and omit steps to implement instruction that is needed for meaningful learning. The main objective, however, for systematically designing any WBI should be the "first-time design" and should satisfy students' learning needs. If the "first-time design" of instruction is planned properly, design critiques will hopefully result in a positive evaluation and the designer promotes meaningful learning.

THE NEED FOR BUILDING BLOCKS! BACK TO BASICS

Plato, as he was supposedly quoted by one of his students, said, "We need to define our terms!" Yes, we need to establish some building blocks.

Communication

The process of communication (Koontz, 1996) is one of the most important aspects as well as one of the most difficult processes of teaching. Without accurate communication, the teacher will not be able to effectively teach students the content of any lesson. Since most of us are fluent in our own language, we take it for granted that the other person understands what we have said. This is not necessarily true. For example, if you want to give verbal instructions to a student to perform some simple task, let's say putting on a jacket, you might start by telling the student to pick up the jacket. The student may pick up the jacket by the sleeve, shoulder, or back, however, you may have been thinking and intended to communicate that the student should pick up the jacket by the collar, thus facilitating a quicker way to put on the jacket. You then must adjust your instruction by telling the student to place his right hand on the collar. Then, step by step, you direct the student as to how to put on the jacket. Communication is a complicated process, and great care must be taken when we speak to our students.

Communication has been defined in many different ways by an array of writers. The definition by Harold Lasswell (1949) is brief and fits our needs. Lasswell defines communication as:

> *Who* said *what* through what *channel* to *whom* with what *effect*.
>
> *Who* is the sender or the person who originates the message. *What* is the content or the message. This message is sent through a selected *channel* or a selected medium or media. *Who* is the receiver or the student and *effect* is the feedback or response we receive from the sender.

The communication model that most effectively fits this definition of communication was designed by Wilber Schramm in the early 1950s and continues to be a working model today. On the left side of the model, we see the *sender*, the originator of the thought, *encoding* or forming a message. The encoding process is the selection of words and putting them into thoughts that will be communicated to the *receiver*, who *decodes* or interprets the message. Between sender and receiver is the *channel* by which the message is transmitted (more on this later). *Feedback* is the response given by the receiver to the sender when the message has been processed.

Feedback may be positive or negative. *Positive feedback* would be the receiver or student correctly interpreting your message and properly

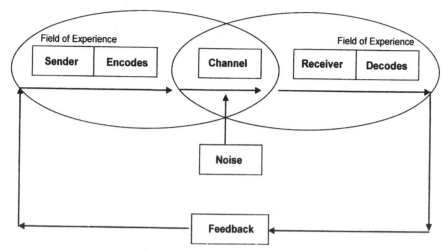

Schramm's Communication Model

responding. *Negative feedback* would be the student interpreting your message and not responding correctly, or the student not interpreting the message correctly and being unable to respond. In the last two cases, the message may have to be reorganized with different cues or more information to obtain positive feedback.

Teachers also receive feedback from their students when any form of homework is evaluated and tests are given. The message is then sent to the original sender and interpreted. Notice that when the teacher receives feedback the roles of the sender and receiver change. The student is the sender and the teacher becomes the receiver. This process is called a *transactional process* because the messages can be called a transaction.

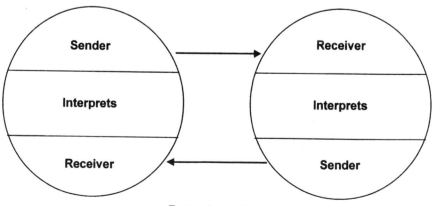

Transactional Model

Transactions continue until the real meaning has been properly interpreted. When we look at the transactional model, we see both sender and receiver changing roles. The receiver interprets the message from the sender and then becomes a sender as they respond back to the original sender who now interprets the message and becomes the receiver. After the message has been correctly interpreted by the receiver, that person once again becomes the sender. This communication cycle continues until both the sender and the receiver understand the transaction.

Referring back to the communication model, the box located just below the channel is labeled *noise*. Noise is anything that interferes with the process of communication. It can be real noise, such as students talking in the hallway, traffic noise near the school, construction that is taking place in the building, and so on. Or it may be mental noise; for example, the students may be thinking about the next assignment, the upcoming exam, and the like. Their minds are not focusing on the present transactions. The noise may also be poorly designed instruction, the improper sequencing of steps taken to solve a problem, or an improper example that is not related to the concept you are teaching. These noises will interfere with the process of communication between you and the student.

The last part of the model includes both the sender and receiver, who have two very large football-like drawings around them. This element is called the *field of experience*. Both you and your students bring to the course of study different fields of experience, but your field of experience is much larger, especially in the course you are teaching. You have studied your field for years and have extensively read the literature and have knowledge of the concepts, theories, and principles. Your students do not have this background. The only part you and the student have in common is where the two parts of the football-like drawing overlap. This represents a very limited field of experience, especially at the beginning of the course. However, as the academic year continues, this field of experience continues to grow. This means that the students are learning what they are supposed to learn.

The *channel* of the communication model is the heart of instructional design—*the intentional selection of a specific channel that will communicate the instruction to the students in such a way as to maximize learning*. In other words, the students will be learning what they are intended to learn and will fulfill the knowledge objectives for the course. In classroom teaching, we may use such teaching methods as lecture-discussions, demonstrations, drill-and-practice, tutorials, cooperative learning groups, and so on. For WBI, we will use different methods, such as analyzing case studies, conducting investigations or participating in simulations, and the like. The proper selection of the appropriate channel is the focus of attention in the instructional design process. *We need to communicate with our students in such a way that noise will be kept to a minimum and the instruction will maximize positive feedback.*

Instruction

We have been using the term *instruction* and now it needs to be defined; that is, we must enlarge our field of experience with an additional term. Surprisingly, many experienced teachers have difficulty explaining this term and confuse it with giving directions for an assignment or test. *Instruction is the deliberate arrangement of information, experiences, and environment to facilitate learning* (Smaldino et al., 2005). Notice that instruction is the deliberate arrangement of specific information or an intentional use of a planned set of experiences for the student to begin to internalize or learn this new information in the learning environment of WBI. Instruction is founded in learning theory.

Teaching

Again, here is a term that has presented some defining problems even to experienced teachers. Even if the individual calls him- or herself a teacher, it has been a problem to accurately define this term. Generally, the first part of the instructional design stage is creating the information to facilitate or to enable learning. Once this part of the design has been completed, it is time to *present or deliver this instruction to the students and engage them in a direct purposeful learning experience.* Teaching, of course, includes the transactions of sending and receiving as illustrated in the transactional model. The methodology used in teaching has been briefly mentioned when defining channel. However, teaching methodologies for WBI needs much more discussion and will be presented in the WBI design model in part 2.

Learning

We know that we have learned our field of study and students who have taken our course in the past have accomplished the knowledge objectives and have learned what they were supposed to have learned from the course. Nevertheless, what is this phenomenon called learning? *Learning*

(Gagné, 1985; Smaldino et al., 2005) is a general term for *a lasting change in our behavior caused by an experience*. It is the development of *new* skills, knowledge, or attitudes (sometimes referred to as SKAs) as we interact with the information and environment. Learning takes place when a *lasting* change of behavior takes place. Notice that emphasis is placed on *new* and *a lasting change of behavior*. If the instruction is not new to us, we have been previously engaged in this material and have already learned the material. Therefore, we are not learning something new but possibly revisiting old information. It also must be a *lasting change of behavior* and the new information must be internalized or become part of us so we can apply and use this information on demand such as completing an assignment or taking a test.

Instructional Design

To begin, instructional design is *a system of procedures for developing course content that is reliable* (Reiser & Dempsey, 2002). Within this somewhat brief definition, several key concepts need to be expanded. First, *system* is one of the most crucial elements in the design process and the understanding of a system will aid the designer throughout the developmental stage.

The assembly of anything that has a number of parts takes time, patience, skill, and a set of properly written instructions (Koontz, 1996). Have you ever attempted to assemble a 10-speed bicycle on Christmas Eve when the pressure is really on? If the assembly instructions are not followed exactly, the bicycle probably will not be usable. All of the parts must be used and adjusted correctly. If just one part of the bicycle is missing or broken—the bicycle will not be functional, for example, if one of the tires is flat, or several spokes in the wheel are bent or broken, or a frame is cracked. However, when all of the parts of the bicycle are installed correctly and properly adjusted, a special effect occurs. This is called a *synergetic effect*, that is to say, *the whole is greater than the sum of all of the parts*. This means that the finished, assembled bicycle is greater than any one of the individual parts. The bicycle then may be ridden as a means of transportation or as a sport and will provide hours and miles of pleasure.

This analogy holds true in the design process when Web-based instruction for an online course is developed. When a design process is implemented, all of the major elements of the model must be used. No major part can be omitted or the design ceases to be a system. All of the parts must work together to obtain the synergetic effect.

The next key term is *develop*, that is to say, the actual designing or writing of the course content in such a way as to create meaningful learning. We'll discuss the concept of developing the instruction much more in part 2 when we discuss the design model.

The last term is used as a statistical term as well as a research term. When we use the term *reliable*, what comes to mind? An employee who always reports to work on time? A car that always starts? Receiving a paycheck on a regular basis? All of these answers are correct. When it comes to designing instruction, we want it to be reliable. The students are learning what they are supposed to be learning, that is, they are achieving the knowledge objectives, and this same instruction can be given to a multiple number of classes with little difference in achievement. We may repeat this instruction multiple number of times and obtain similar results.

E-instructional Design

This new term needs to be defined. It contains the same meaning as instructional design, that is, a system of procedures for developing course content that is reliable. However, e-instructional design specifically refers to instructional design procedures that are used to design distance education courses or Web-based instruction placed on the Web.

ID MODEL BASICS—THE ADDIE MODEL

When reviewing exiting ID models, we find that literally dozens of models have been designed for various types of classroom instruction (Gustafson & Branch, 1997). All of these variations of instructional models have five common core elements: analysis, design, development, implementation, and evaluation (ADDIE).

Analysis refers to a needs assessment, that is, what the students need to learn or do as a result of the instruction (Dick, Carey, & Carey, 2001). You determine what skills, knowledge, or attitudes the student needs to acquire to accomplish the task he or she is to perform. In the *design* stage you write the knowledge objectives that may be evaluated in some measurable form as well as creating the instruction and selecting media (Smaldino et al., 2005), including exercises and assignments that will accomplish the objectives. During the *development* stage the instructor and student materials are prepared which have been determined by the design requirements (Morrison, Ross, & Kemp, 2004). The *implementation* stage (also called

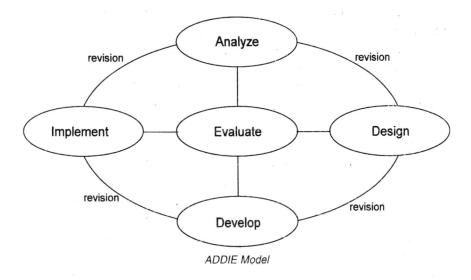

ADDIE Model

the teaching stage) is the delivery of the instruction to the student using a selected channel that has been determined appropriate for the design. Finally, *evaluation* of the instruction, both *formative*, that is, during the time the instruction is being prepared, and *summative*, at the end of the course, is needed to determine its effectiveness (Dick et al., 2001). Evaluation of instruction is continuous in the ADDIE model and is considered the core of instructional design. Much of the formative evaluation will be regularly performed as you make design decisions as to content and hands-on tasks needed for the students to accomplish the knowledge objectives and then the selection of the best way to implement the instruction. Summative evaluation is generally conducted after the course has been completed and can give you valuable data as to both the positive and negative aspects of the course. There may also be negative feedback concerning improvements that are needed.

BASIC CHARACTERISTICS OF INSTRUCTIONAL DESIGN

The ADDIE model represents the basic elements generally found in all instructional design models. Some basic elements should be found in the process of designing instruction.

Instructional design:

1. is student-centered;
2. is oriented toward knowledge objectives;

3. has practical performance; and
4. is directed toward student outcomes that are observable and can be measured. (Reiser & Dempsey, 2002)

Student-Centered

The focal point of all designed instruction is the performance of the student or learner. The process of designing instruction and implementation of this instruction is the means to the end for student performance. The design process concentrates on the skills, knowledge, and attitudes that must be learned to accomplish the knowledge objectives. When you continually concentrate on what the student will get out of the lesson, you will automatically include the necessary content for the instruction.

Oriented Toward Knowledge Objectives

The content to be learned in individual lessons as well as the entire course is driven by the objectives you design. This is the focal point of the lesson. It guides the student as a rudder guides a ship or steering wheel guides a car. Without this absolute and necessary knowledge objective, the students will not and cannot learn what they are supposed to learn.

Practical Performance

The process of memorizing, recalling facts, names, or steps, is the lowest form of learning (Koontz, 1996). Sometimes, out of necessity, students must learn the basics of your course content—certain terms, concepts, steps, etc.—in this way. Once completed, however, you will want your students to move up the ladder of learning and to make their performance responses in accordance with what will be found in the workforce as much as possible.

Directed Toward Observable and Measurable Student Outcomes

As we will learn more about in part 2, any knowledge objective that cannot be observed or measured, either by qualitative methods (how well the student performed) or quantitative methods (how much the student obtained), cannot be used. The heart of instructional design is the feedback you can obtain from students to enable you to judge their level of learning.

This type of feedback is obtained by assignments, class performance, and tests. If you cannot obtain tangible results or feedback from your students, there is no basis on which any type of grade or evaluation may be applied.

DISTANCE EDUCATION, DISTANCE LEARNING, OR E-LEARNING?

More terms need to be defined and discussed. You will notice some textbooks and articles use the term *distance education* while others use the term *distance learning*. One textbook has a chapter titled "Distance Learning." The first knowledge objective stated in the advance organizer of the text states: *Define distance education*. Confusing? Yes, to some extent. Both of these terms are used regularly. Technically, however, we probably do not teach specific learning skills or how to learn specific subject content (Moore & Kearsley, 1996). These are skills we assume our students already have. Therefore, to some extent, distance learning is an improper term to use. In distance education, however, we provide a very broad base of organized instruction for students to learn specific subject content. However, both terms are used interchangeably in the literature.

Still another term that has crept into our instructional design vocabulary is *e-learning*. If you recall, the letter *e* was used with the term e-mail signifying that mail was electronically sent via the World Wide Web. This being the case, it seems reasonable that e-learning would be defined as electronic learning from a Web-based course and would carry the same meaning as distance education and distance learning.

For our purposes we will use the distance education definition provided by Moore and Kearsley (1996) as a working definition:

> Distance education is *planned learning* that normally occurs in a *different place* from teaching and as a result requires special techniques of course design, *special instructional techniques*, *special methods of communication* by electronic and other technology, as well as special organizational and administrative arrangements.

Notice the definition stresses certain terms such as *planned learning*. Instruction for WBI should not be "just-in-time" learning experiences. Web-based learning experiences must be carefully designed and reinforced by learning theory, since the majority of the learning will occur in a *different place* from the teaching. Because distance learning contains a different set of variables than that of the classroom, such as the separation of teacher and student, delayed feedback, and so on, *special instructional techniques* of course design must be employed to ensure that meaningful learning does take place using a variety of communication techniques to provide the necessary positive reinforcement needed by the student. In addition, special methods of communication, such as e-mail, chat rooms, message boards, or even the conventional telephone, may be used.

Distance education may also be *synchronous*, that is, the teacher is conducting a live class or a class in real time via the Internet and interacting with the class during a scheduled time. The class may also be *asynchronous*, having the instruction prepared in advance for students to access at their convenience without the teacher interacting with them in real time. In this case, you have already produced the instruction and the students may access the sessions at their convenience. Feedback from asynchronous Web-based courses may be obtained primarily using e-mail, chat rooms, message boards, and the like. However, we should not forget some of the traditional forms of communication such as a telephone or even having the class come together at specified times during the semester or quarter.

WEB-BASED INSTRUCTION

One last term that needs to be identified is Web-based instruction (WBI). Li (2003) defined it as a "hypermedia-based instructional program, which utilizes the attributes and resources of the World Wide Web to create a meaningful learning environment where learning is fostered and supported." This is a formal way to say we are using software that permits us to use a computer to design and deliver instruction, using text, data, sound, and video in such a way that a student can access it on the World Wide Web.

SUMMARY

Traditionally, classroom instruction has been designed using proven ID models specifically designed for the traditional way of teaching. The unique nature of distance education requires a new model for this new way of teaching. The student is geographically separated from the teacher, feedback may be indirect or delayed, and, for the most part, the student independently and in isolation interacts with the instruction. The importance of accurately communicating instruction using a "first-time design" procedure increases the probability that students will learn what they are supposed to learn. In effect, using appropriate design techniques will tend to maximize student learning in a reduced amount of time. When positive student feedback is received, it reinforces that the appropriate design and teaching technique was communicated to the student.

Basic to all instruction are the analysis, design, development, implementation, and evaluation steps found in the ADDIE model. These steps, when used, create a synergetic effect. All of the steps must be used to create a systems approach to the design of instruction. When one or more of the steps is omitted, the system no longer exists. Also basic to instructional models are the characteristics of student-centered instruction, oriented toward knowledge objectives, having practical performance, and directed toward outcomes that are observable and measurable.

Although *distance learning* is probably the most common term applied to online courses, *distance education* is technically the more precise term. When students take online courses, we do not teach them how to learn the subject content through distance. The assumption made is that the students already have the skills to learn. Distance education is the process of providing broad curricula using the World Wide Web. As it most frequently happens, we tend to adopt a term that is less complicated and more readily understood by the majority.

"New wine in new wineskins" is a metaphor that illustrates that the new Web-based instruction we prepare for our online courses must be placed in a new model to accommodate the differences in the way we teach and in the way our students learn.

This handbook is intended to give you specific information concerning the process of course design, instructional techniques, and a selection of methods to implement your instruction in distance learning.

In distance education, you can take the teacher out of the classroom, but you cannot take the teacher out of teaching.

REFERENCES

Dick, W., Carey, L., & Carey, J. (2001). *The systematic design of instruction.* (5th ed.). New York: Addison-Wesley Educational Publishers.

Gagné, R. (1985). *The conditions of learning and theory of instruction.* (4th ed.). New York: Holt, Rinehart and Winston.

Gustafson, K., & Branch, R. (1997). *Survey of instructional development models.* (3rd ed.). Syracuse, NY: ERIC Clearinghouse on Information & Technology.

Koontz, F. R. (1996). *Media and technology in the classroom.* (5th ed.). Dubuque, IA: Kendall/Hunt.

Lasswell, H. D. (1949). *Communication defined.* Wikipedia Free Encyclopedia. Retrieved March 15, 2003 from www.wikipedia.org/wiki/Harold_Lasswell.

Li, H. (2003). *Investigation of a new instructional design model for Web-based instruction (WBI): A Delphi study.* Unpublished doctoral dissertation, The University of Toledo, Toledo, OH.

Moore, M. G., & Kearsley, G. (1996). *Distance education: A systems view.* Belmont, CA: Wadsworth.

Morrison, G., Ross, S., & Kemp, J. (2004). *Designing effective instruction.* (4th ed.). Hoboken, NJ: John Wiley & Sons.

Reiser, R., & Dempsey, J. (Eds.). (2002). *Trends and issues in instructional design and technology.* Upper Saddle River, NJ: Merrill/Prentice Hall.

Smaldino, S., Russell, J., Heinich, R., & Molenda, M. (2005). *Instructional technology and media for learning.* (8th ed.). Upper Saddle River, NJ: Pearson/Merrill/Prentice Hall.

Sun, X. (2001). *An investigation of instructional models for Web-based instruction.* Unpublished doctoral dissertation, The University of Toledo, Toledo, OH.

CHAPTER 2

Learning Theory

CHAPTER OUTLINE

What Is Learning and Learning Theory?
Behavioral Theories
Cognitive Theories and Gagné's Theory of Instruction
   Gagné's Domains of Learning and Conditions of Learning
      Intellectual Skills
      Verbal Information
   Conditions of Learning
      Attitudes
      Motor Skills
      Cognitive Strategies
   Nine Events of Instruction
Constructivism
Problem Solving and Online Learning
Summary
References

KNOWLEDGE OBJECTIVES

At the end of this chapter, you should be able to:

1. Compare the relationship between learning theory and instructional design.
2. Analyze the influence of behavioral theories on online learning
3. Define the domains of learning by Gagné.
4. Describe, with examples, the nine events of instruction and how are they related to online instruction.
5. Determine how constructivism affects Web-based instruction.
6. Explain why problem solving is important in online learning.

LEXICON

Terms to know:

attitude	learning
behavioral theory	learning theory
cognitive strategies	motor skills
cognitive theory	online learning
constructivism	problem solving
domains of learning	verbal information
intellectual skill	

> *"I never teach my pupils; I only attempt to provide the conditions in which they can learn."*

> —*Albert Einstein*

In 1927, Ivan Pavlov, a Russian physiologist, noticed an interesting phenomenon. Whenever it was time to feed the dogs in the laboratory, the dogs began to salivate. Interestingly enough, the dogs salivated even without seeing the food, simply upon seeing or hearing the footsteps of the keeper.

This story is the famous experiment of classical conditioning, and Pavlov is considered to be one of the influential behaviorists. Many other educational psychologists founded different ways of examining learning and teaching. In this chapter, behaviorism, cognitive theory, constructivism, and Gagné's conditions of learning will be addressed.

WHAT IS LEARNING AND LEARNING THEORY?

Different educational psychologists view the concept of learning differently. Behaviorists believe that learning is nothing but change in behavior; cognitive theorists view learning as a process; and social learning theorists view learning process as interaction/observation in social context (Merriam & Caffarella, 1991). One thing they have in common is that they all assume that "instruction will bring about learning" and, based on this assumption, instructional designers use theories as guidance to design effective instruction to bring about maximum learning (Driscoll, 2002).

Bloom (1956) defines three domains in which learning occurs: the cognitive, psychomotor, and affective domains. According to Bloom, six types of learning are in the cognitive domain, each one building on the previous one. These include knowledge, comprehension, application, analysis, synthesis, and evaluation.

Bloom's definition of learning is rooted in behaviorism. Cognitive theorists would not agree with the definition because it lacks attention to mental processing and the creation of new mental constructs, and constructivists would be concerned because of the absence of notions of knowledge construction. However, it at least defines learning more clearly, allowing the discussion of the type of learning that an online learning environment attempts to support.

Online learning, as a subset of learning in general, is a relatively new concept in recent years. It refers to any learning or teaching that takes place via a computer network (Kearsley, 1999). Wilson's (1997) taxonomy of computer applications organizes computerized learning environments into three categories: (1) computer microworlds, (2) classroom-based learning environments, and (3) open virtual environments. Any of these may be online, but online learning does not include learning that is delivered via the computer without networking requirements, such as stand-alone drill-and-practice software, applications developed for CD-ROM, or applications accessed via broadcast networks such as radio, broadcast television, or satellite systems. Online learning in higher education covers only those applications developed and accessed through the World Wide Web.

Wilson (1997) has described three functions of a good educational theory. First, it helps us to envision new worlds. In the new online learning environment, we do need theory to help us envision how instruction can best utilize the enhanced communication, information retrieval, and management capability provided by the Web. Second, a good theory helps us to make things. We need theories of online learning that help us to invest our time and limited resources most effectively. Third, Wilson argues that a good theory keeps us honest. Good theory builds upon what is already known and helps us to interpret and plan for the unknown.

Theories help us make sense out of the world and provide a framework for behaving intelligently. Learning theory helps students to learn more efficiently and more effectively. Learning theory is used to guide our daily teaching. That is why professional teaching really means "using research to guide practice" (Joyce, Weil, & Calhoun, 2004).

BEHAVIORAL THEORIES

Among the frequently asked questions by faculty in higher education are: "How do my college students learn since everybody has a different learning style? What is the best way to teach during an online course?"

Behavioral theories study animal and human learning and focus on objectively observable behaviors and discount mental activities. Behavior theorists define learning as nothing more than the acquisition of new behavior.

This theory is relatively simple to understand because it relies only on observable behavior and describes several universal laws of behavior. It explains learning of skills and attitudes. Its positive and negative reinforcement techniques can be very effective. Behaviorism is often used by teachers, who reward or punish students for behavior modifications (Lefrançois, 1991).

Certainly, some evidence illustrates that learning theory has been applied into educational environments. Maddux, Johnson, and Willis (2001) considered behaviorism to have been the dominant theory of learning in North America for most of the twentieth century. When computers were introduced to the classrooms of many schools for the first time, behavioral theories were very popular. The famous innovation of programmed instruction was one of the examples based on behavioral theories.

In summary, behaviorists believe that learning is nothing but change in behavior. Learning occurs when stimuli in external environment are present. The purpose of education is to produce behavioral change in desired direction. The educator's role is to arrange an environment to elicit the desired response (Merriam & Caffarella, 1991).

COGNITIVE THEORIES AND GAGNÉ'S THEORY OF INSTRUCTION

Cognitive theorists view the learning process as an internal mental process (including insight, information processing, memory, and perception). The purpose of education is to develop capacity and skills needed to learn better. So it requires the educators to structure content of learning activity (Merriam & Caffarella, 1991).

Many types of information-processing models in the cognitive family emphasize ways of enhancing the human being's innate drive to make sense of the world by acquiring and organizing data, sensing problems and generating solutions to them, and developing concepts and language for conveying them. Some models provide the learner with information and concepts, some emphasize concept formation and hypothesis testing, and still others generate creative thinking. A few are designed to enhance general intellectual ability. Many information-processing models are useful for studying the self and society, and thus, for achieving the personal and social goals of education (Joyce, Weil, & Calhoun, 2004).

Gagné's Domains of Learning and Conditions of Learning

Gagné (1985) classified learning into five major categories: intellectual skills, verbal information, attitudes, motor skills, and cognitive strategies.

In essence, these five domains represent outcomes of the learning process. What makes Gagné's instructional theory particularly useful is his analysis of the conditions that foster learning the capabilities represented by each of the five domains. Knowledge of the conditions is particularly valuable to the design of instructional strategies on online instruction.

Intellectual Skills

Intellectual skills refer to the outcomes of learning. In one sense, these skills are the outcomes of the learning process described by other learning theorists.

Verbal Information

A great deal of school learning that has caused teachers' concern is verbal information (Lefrançois, 1991). It is more or less what people generally explain as knowledge. A typical characteristic of verbal knowledge is that it can be expressed in a sentence.

Conditions of Learning

Many of the conditions Gagné described as desirable external conditions for the acquisition of verbal information are validated by more recent cognitive research (as in Glaser & Bassok, 1989). Thus, Gagné mentioned the importance of advance organizers and meaningful context. He also suggested using instructional aids for motivation and retention.

Attitudes

Educators throughout the world have a number of grand goals: to teach students knowledge and good citizenship. Conditions in this category include models, reinforcement, and verbal guidance.

Motor Skills

Motor skills involve the execution of sequences of controlled muscular movements. Writing, walking, and talking are all classified as motor skills. Conditions in this domain involve models, verbal directions, reinforcement (knowledge of results), and practice.

Cognitive Strategies

Cognitive strategies refer to the complex and highly personal strategies that govern how we pay attention, how we study, organize, and recall information. Suggested conditions for facilitating outcomes in this category include frequent presentation of novel and/or challenging problems.

In summary, Gagné's classification of domains of learning and of external conditions that appear to facilitate these outcomes has been described above. Knowledge of both conditions and outcomes can be of value in helping the teacher and instructional designer to arrive at appropriate instructional strategy.

Nine Events of Instruction

In addition to conditions of learning that are unique to each learning outcome, certain conditions of learning facilitate the process of learning in general. Gagné conceived the nine events of instruction as learning conditions to support internal processes such as attention, encoding, and decoding. The nine events of instruction are as follows, with example procedures given on designing a computer-based lesson:

1. *Gaining attention.* Present initial operating instructions on screen, including some displays that change second by second.
2. *Informing the learner of the objectives.* State in simple terms what the student will have accomplished once he or she has learned.
3. *Stimulating recall of prior learning.* Recall concepts previously learned.
4. *Presenting the stimulus.* Present a definition of the concept.
5. *Providing learning guidance.* Provide a cue or strategy to promote encoding.
6. *Eliciting performance.* Present examples on what is being learned.
7. *Providing feedback.* Give information about correct and incorrect responses.
8. *Assessing performance.* Present a new set of concept instances and noninstances; ask questions requiring answers.
9. *Enhancing retention and transfer.* Present additional concept instances, varied in form. (Gagné, Briggs, & Wager, 1988)

Gagné's nine events of instruction is a commonly used instructional design procedure when designing Web-based instruction (Li, 2003). Though it was originally created for traditional classroom setting, it is still used by many instructional designers when designing online instruction.

CONSTRUCTIVISM

Constructivism is a philosophy of learning founded on the premise that by reflecting on our experiences, we construct our own understanding of the world we live in. Each of us generates our own "rules" and "mental models," which we use to make sense of our experiences. Learning, therefore, is simply the process of adjusting our mental models to accommodate new experiences (Funderstanding, 2001).

Several guiding principles of constructivism are detailed below:

1. Learning is a search for meaning. Therefore, learning must start with the issues around which students are actively trying to construct meaning.
2. Meaning requires understanding wholes as well as parts, and parts must be understood in the context of wholes. Therefore, the learning process focuses on primary concepts, not isolated facts.
3. In order to teach well, we must understand the mental models that students use to perceive the world and the assumptions they make to support those models.
4. The purpose of learning is for an individual to construct his or her own meaning, not just to memorize the "right" answers and regurgitate someone else's meaning. Since education is inherently interdisciplinary, the only valuable way to measure learning is to make the assessment part of the learning process, ensuring it provides students with information on the quality of their learning.

Constructivism calls for the elimination of a standardized curriculum. Instead, it promotes using curricula customized to the students' prior knowledge. Also, it emphasizes hands-on problem solving (Bruner, 1966). Here, the student has the benefit of integrating previous experiences, perceptions, and internal representations of knowledge with every new learning opportunity. The learner uses existing cognitive structures to select and modify information, build hypotheses, and make sound decisions (Kearsley, 1999).

Under the theory of constructivism, educators focus on making connections between facts and fostering new understanding in students. Instructors tailor their teaching strategies to student responses and encourage students to analyze, interpret, and predict information. Teachers also rely heavily on open-ended questions and promote extensive dialogue among students. Constructivism calls for the elimination of grades and standardized testing; instead, assessment becomes part of the learning process so that students play a larger role in judging their own progress.

As far as instruction is concerned, the instructor should try and encourage students to discover principles by themselves. The instructor and student should engage in an active dialogue (i.e., Socratic learning). The task of the instructor is to translate information to be learned into a format appropriate to the learner's current state of understanding. The curriculum should be organized in a spiral manner so that students continually build upon what they have already learned.

Brooks and Brooks (1993) make a strong and powerful argument for the "constructivist classroom." They outline the characteristics of the constructivist classroom, stating that creation of this classroom is the result of incorporating some guiding principles of constructivism. These guiding principles are:

1. Posing problems of emerging relevance.
2. Structuring learning around primary concepts.
3. Seeking and valuing student's point of view.
4. Adapting curriculum to address student's suppositions.
5. Assessing student learning in the context of teaching. (Brooks & Brooks, 1993).

Brooks and Brooks are referring to a more traditional classroom setting; however, many of these guiding principles are applicable for WBI.

Although constructivism is not a high-level design theory, instructional designers inspired by constructivist ideas have attempted to explain what constructivism might mean in the context of online environments. The implementation of a constructive environment online can be done through the process of discovery learning. Given an authentic activity, a Web-based learner has numerous tools available that support the discovery process. Toomey and Ketterer (1995) further assert that multimedia enforces a learner-centered, teacher-guided approach to the teaching/ learning process. This constructive approach is necessary in Web-based instruction because students are forced to access, retrieve, reconstruct, adapt, and organize information in a way that is meaningful to their learning. Clearly, the computer coupled with multimedia is a powerful cognitive tool (Bruner, 1966).

PROBLEM SOLVING AND ONLINE LEARNING

Problem solving is not as easy to define as it may sound. Jonassen (2000) defines problem solving as follows: "Problem solving involves systematically pursuing a goal, which is usually the solution of a problem that a situation presents" (p. 30). He adds that problem solving is perhaps the most common complex thinking skill, and identifies the following steps:

1. Sensing the problem
2. Researching the problem
3. Formulating the problem
4. Finding alternatives
5. Choosing the solution
6. Building acceptance

If asked, most educators would agree that one essential goal of education is the development of students who are effective problem solvers for the information age. Problem solving has long been emphasized as the purpose of education. Gagné (1985) proposes that "the central point of education is to teach people to think, to use their rational powers, to become better problem solvers." Problem solving is considered among the higher-order thinking skills. It involves the application of several rules to a problem not encountered before by the learner. Problem solving involves selecting the correct rules and applying them in combination.

Even though it is considered the most important type of learning both in schools and in life, the field of instructional design has unfortunately largely ignored problem solving (Jonassen, 2002). Some researchers take the initiative to address the issue. Savery and Duffy's (1996) problem-based design principles outlines the elements to pedagogically sound instruction: (1) learning should be relevant; (2) instructional goals should be consistent with learner's goals; (3) cognitive demands and tasks in the learning environment should be consistent with cognitive demands and tasks for the environment for which the learner is being prepared; (4) the teacher's role is to challenge the students' thinking; (5) the students' role is to challenge the students' thinking; (6) students' ideas should be tested against alternative views through social negotiation and collaborative learning groups; and (7) reflection on the learning process should be encouraged.

Problem-based learning is learning that occurs through the process of defining, understanding, and solving a problem. For meaningful learning to occur, problems must be authentic and contextualized. Properly designed Web-based learning can support the problem-based learning process (Collins, 1997).

The problem-based learning curriculum consists of two parts. First, the student must be made aware of the learning goal. The teacher is responsible for clearly identifying the lessons to be learned and establishing expected outcomes (Ritchie & Hoffman, 1997). This can be easily accomplished in an informational Web page linking to other Web resources. Second, a learning sequence, consisting of problem-based learning cycles, must be developed (Duffy & Cunningham, 1996). Students are encouraged to work collaboratively, with each other and with the experts, through each of the cycles. The Internet supports this communication and allows for threaded discussions so that problem solving can be broken into tasks. The learning sequence is supported by a facilitator who can guide the discussion and assist students in moving through the problem-based learning cycles until project completion.

Web-based instruction is currently a popular method for delivering college courses. WBI has the potential to offer a rich and stimulating educational environment (Windschitl, 1998). The World Wide Web provides both teacher and students with numerous learning opportunities by allowing students to learn and develop at their own pace, enhancing writing and communication skills, developing higher-order problem-solving skills, and nurturing critical reflection (Peck & Dorricott, 1994).

There are challenges for incorporating valid pedagogical principles into Web-based instruction: "[S]imply publishing a World Wide Web page with links to other digital resources does not constitute instruction" (Ritchie & Hoffman, 1997). Schneider (1994) states that the instruction must be grounded in educational theory and not solely based on educational content or on the technology used to deliver the information. While traditional learning theory could evolve with time as educational technologies become more sophisticated, most traditional learning theories still facilitate the transfer and knowledge and promote learning.

SUMMARY

Learning has always been the focus in education. In recent years, online learning became a popular topic particularly in higher education, with the widespread use of the Internet and the World Wide Web. The new paradigm of Web-based instruction calls for the need to incorporate learning theory and sound instructional design principles because "simply publishing a World Wide Web page with links to other digital resources does not constitute instruction" (Ritchie & Hoffman, 1997).

Different families of learning theories view learning differently. Behavioral theory views learning as change of behavior, while cognitive theory views learning as internal process (Merriam & Caffarella, 1991). As an example of cognitive family, Gagné (1985) classified learning into five major categories (intellectual skills, verbal information, attitudes, motor skills, and cognitive strategies). Meanwhile, he analyzed conditions that foster each type of learning. His nine events of instruction are still commonly used to design Web-based instruction (Li, 2003). In addition to behavioral and cognitive theories, constructivism brings a new look to instruction. Building on their prior knowledge, students construct their learning through hands-on problem solving (Bruner, 1966). Lastly, problem-solving strategy requires students to pursue a goal and promotes complex thinking skills (Jonassen, 2000).

Instruction should be grounded in educational theory and not solely based on educational content or on the technology used to deliver the information (Schneider, 1994). Today, the instructional setting and the technologies used in classrooms have become more and more advanced. Traditional learning theories, however, still facilitate learning and serve as the guideline for instruction and instructional design.

REFERENCES

Bloom, B. (Ed.). (1956). *Taxonomy of educational objectives: The classification of educational goals: Handbook I, cognitive domain*. New York: Longmans, Green.

Brooks, J., & Brooks, M. (1993). *In search of understanding: The case for constructivist classrooms*. Alexandria, VA: Association for Supervision and Curriculum Development.

Bruner, J. (1966). *Toward a theory of instruction*. Cambridge, MA: Belknap Press of Harvard University.

Collins, B. (1997). Supporting project-based collaborative learning via a World Wide Web environment. In B. H. Khan (Ed.), *Web-based instruction* (pp. 213–219). Englewood Cliffs, NJ: Educational Technology Publications.

Driscoll, M. (2002). Psychological foundations of instructional design. In R. Reiser and J. Dempsey (Eds.), *Trends and issues in instructional design and technology* (pp. 57–69). Upper Saddle River, NJ: Merrill/Prentice Hall.

Duffy, T., & Cunningham, D. (1996). Constructivism: implications for the design and delivery of instruction. In D. H. Jonassen (Ed.), *Handbook of research for educational communications and technology* (pp. 170–198). New York: Macmillan Library Reference USA.

Funderstanding (2001). About learning. Retrieved January 10, 2005, from http://www .funderstanding.com/about_learning.cfm.com

Gagné, R. (1985). *The conditions of learning and theory of instruction.* (4th ed.). New York: Holt, Rinehart and Winston.

Gagné, R., Briggs, L., & Wager, W. (1988). *Principles of instructional design.* (3rd ed.). Fort Worth, TX: Holt, Rinehart and Winston.

Glaser, R., & Bassok, M. (1989). Learning theory and the study of instruction. *Annual review of psychology, 40,* 631–666.

Jonassen, D. (2000). *Computers as mind tools for schools: Engaging critical thinking.* (2nd ed.) Upper Saddle River, NJ: Merrill.

Jonassen, D. (2002). Integration of problem solving into instructional design. In R. Reiser and J. Dempsey (Eds.), *Trends and issues in instructional design and technology* (pp. 107–120). Upper Saddle River, NJ: Merrill/Prentice Hall.

Joyce, B., Weil, M., & Calhoun, E. (2004). *Models of teaching.* (7th ed.). Boston: Allyn and Bacon.

Kearsley, G. (1999). Explorations in learning & instruction: The theory into practice database. Retrieved February 10, 2005, from http://tip.psychology.org/.

Lefrançois, G. (1991). *Psychology for teaching: A bear always, usually, sometimes, rarely, never, always faces the front—will not commit himself just now.* (7th ed.). Belmont, CA: Wadsworth.

Li, H. (2003). *Investigation of a new instructional design model for Web-based instruction (WBI): A Delphi study.* Unpublished doctoral dissertation, The University of Toledo, Toledo, OH.

Maddux, C., Johnson, D., & Willis, J. (2001). *Educational computing: Learning with tomorrow's technologies.* (3rd ed.). Boston: Allyn and Bacon.

Merriam, S., & Caffarella, R. (1991). *Learning in adulthood: A comprehensive guide.* San Francisco: Jossey-Bass.

Peck, K., & Dorricott, D. (1994). Why use technology? *Educational Leadership,* April, 11–14.

Ritchie, D., & Hoffman, B. (1997). Incorporating instructional design principles with the World Wide Web. In B. H. Khan (Ed.), *Web-based instruction* (pp. 135–138). Englewood Cliffs, NJ: Educational Technology Publications.

Savery, J., & Duffy, T. (1996). Problem-based learning: An instructional model and its constructivist framework. In B. Wilson (Ed.), *Constructivist learning environments: Case studies in instructional design* (pp. 135–148). Englewood Cliffs, NJ: Educational Technology Publications.

Schneider, D. (1994). *Teaching and learning with Internet tools: A position paper.* Paper presented at the Workshop on Teaching and Learning with the Web at the First International Conference on the World Wide Web, Geneva, Switzerland.

Toomey, R., & Ketterer, K. (1995). Using multimedia as a cognitive tool. *Journal of Research on Computing in Education, 27*(4), 473–482.

Wilson, B. (1997). Thoughts on theory in educational technology. *Educational Technology, 37*(1), 22–26.

Windschitl, M. (1998). The WWW and classroom research: What path should we take? *Educational Researcher, 27*(1), 28–33.

CHAPTER 3

Distance Learning Research Findings

CHAPTER OUTLINE

Brief History and Definition
The Online Learner
Andragogy and Pedagogy
Attitudes of Learners
The Online Instructor
The Need to Follow a Model
Objectives
Summary
References

KNOWLEDGE OBJECTIVES

At the end of this chapter, you should be able to:

1. Define distance education.
2. Explain the characteristics of online learners.
3. Define and discuss the concepts of andragogy and pedagogy.
4. Discuss attitudes of online learners.
5. Identify and discuss issues concerning online instructors.
6. Discuss the importance of educational objectives.
7. Explain the need to follow an instructional design model.

LEXICON

Terms to know:

andragogy
distance education
distance learning
feedback
information navigation

instruction
instructional design (ID)
objectives
pedagogy
teaching

"Progress is impossible without change; and those who cannot change their minds cannot change anything."

—*George Bernard Shaw*

BRIEF HISTORY AND DEFINITION

To those of us who find ourselves employed at a college or university early in the twenty-first century, it is clear that we are living in a time of great change. The boundaries of our classrooms are changing. The methods and technologies we use to deliver instruction are constantly changing. Most importantly, our students and their educational needs are also changing. As educators and administrators at colleges and universities across the country, we are finding out that in order to meet the demands of students, it is sometimes necessary to move beyond the walls of the academy to provide students with the education they both need and desire.

Technological advances in telecommunications and computers have helped make educational opportunities more accessible and convenient for many students. As the needs of students change, institutions often find it necessary to break the conventional educational paradigm in order to meet these needs. Much more emphasis is being placed on distance education programs, particularly Web-based instruction.

Distance education is defined by Moore and Kearsley (1996) as follows:

> Distance education is planned learning that normally occurs in a different place from teaching and as a result requires special techniques of course design, special instructional techniques, special methods of communication by electronic and other technology, as well as special organizational and administrative arrangements.

Moore and Kearsley are quick to point out that distance education is much more complex than simply integrating technology in a conventional classroom. Careful planning and a systematic design approach, which the ASSIST-Me model provides, is essential to make sure that the needs of the students are continuously being met in an ever-changing environment.

While the emergence of the World Wide Web is certainly a recent phenomenon that seems like a relatively new innovation to many educators today, the underlying concept of distance delivery of instruction is more than a century old. The earliest instructional delivery method, originally established in the late 1800s in Germany, was called correspondence study. Shorthand instruction was delivered via the postal system in order for students to learn at home. Willis (1994) states that "present day distance education has its roots in early university correspondence and extension programs designed primarily to educate students via paper based processes."

We have certainly come a long way from the correspondence courses. During the twentieth century, distance education delivery systems began to move away from correspondence study and turn to broadcast technologies as the preferred delivery method. As media and communication technology such as radio, television, and computers developed, they were often assimilated into the delivery process, assuming the role of primary carrier (Willis, 1994).

The changes during the 1990s and into the twenty-first century have certainly made distance education, particularly online learning, more attractive to both students and institutions. Greg Kearsley (2000) attributes the popularity of Web-based learning to three key factors: "the easy availability of computers and networks; the presence of mature, motivated students capable of independent study; and faculty who are competent in using network technologies required to offer such courses."

Downes (1998) adds the perspective that online learning provides learners with personalized instruction that is more efficient than traditional classroom learning:

> Classroom education is in many ways wasteful. Material is reviewed for thirty students when in fact only five need review. New material presented is absorbed by half the students, but is beyond the capacity of the other half. That time in class which is spent by a student unproductively . . . is eliminated through personalized instruction.

For these reasons, online learning and instruction has become much more attractive to students and faculty, and this trend is likely to continue into the twenty-first century as the technology used to deliver instruction continues to evolve.

While the methods of delivery tend to evolve, the primary object of distance learning remains focused on the need to provide quality instruction to the learners. Therefore, it is essential that an instructional design model, such as the ASSIST-Me model presented in this book, is employed to ensure that instruction meets the needs of the learners. Gustafson and Branch (2002) define instructional design as "a system of procedures for developing education and training programs in a consistent and reliable fashion. Instructional design is a complex process that is creative, active, and iterative." The ASSIST-Me model provides the framework to ensure that the design of instruction follows a systematic process and that the needs of the learners are met.

THE ONLINE LEARNER

In the instruction design process, it is essential to ascertain what exactly we know about adult learners. What is their profile? Understanding the needs of the learner is a fundamental instructional design concept. While many researchers have attempted to create profiles of online learners, this task has proved daunting simply because, like the technologies involved in online learning, the students themselves are also an ever-changing, dynamic population. Traditionally, online learners are assumed to be adults with various levels of personal and professional commitments. Thompson (1998) indicates "that although distance learners share broad demographic and situational characteristics, no concrete evidence exists to indicate that this group is homogeneous and unchanging" (cited in Dabbagh & Bannan-Ritland, 2005).

Quite honestly, I can say from experience that it is the younger students who generally possess the requisite skills needed to succeed in an online environment. Students are acquiring information navigation, a new type of literacy skill that is critical for online learning: "Information navigation goes beyond text and image literacy, requiring learners to navigate 'through confusing complex information spaces and feel comfortable doing so'" (Dabbagh & Bannan-Ritland, 2005).

However, if we are operating under the assumption that the typical distance learner is an adult with varying levels of commitments, we must determine how to best address the needs of this population, whose needs differ from those of traditional students. I would have to agree with the assumption that, at least to some extent, adult students learn differently than younger students, and that different strategies must be considered when designing adult-centered online instruction.

Since distance education results in such a personal learning experience, understanding the characteristics of adult learners is of extreme importance. Simonson, Smaldino, Albright, and Zvacek (2003) conclude that "[s]uccessful distance education learners tend traditionally to be abstract learners who are intrinsically motivated and possess internal locus of control." Further, according to Minton and Willet (2003), "Distance education caters to the non-traditional student and is not intended for every student. The fact that it [distance education] is not appropriate for every student is widely accepted." In acknowledging this fact, it then must be determined how adult online learners learn best.

ANDRAGOGY AND PEDAGOGY

Knowles (1980) originally defined *andragogy* as "the art and science of helping adults learn, in contrast to pedagogy as the art and science of teaching children." However, elementary and secondary teachers found that andragogical concepts, in certain situations, were producing superior learning. Therefore, andragogy can be viewed as "simply another model of assumptions about learners to be used alongside the pedagogical model of assumptions, thereby providing two alternative models for testing out assumptions as to their 'fit' with particular situations." Some of the andragogical assumptions seem to be quite accurate when dealing with a population often labeled non-traditional.

This does not mean that some pedagogical strategies cannot be used effectively in online instruction geared toward adults. Rather, these two theories represent different ends of a learning spectrum. Still, experience has proven that many of the assumptions that are attributed to adults usually hold true and that andragogical strategies tend to work better than pedagogical ones.

One assumption, presented by Knowles (1980) regarding the concept of the learner, is particularly accurate:

> It is a normal aspect of the process of maturation for a person to move from dependency toward increasing self-directedness, but at different rates for different people and in different dimensions of life. . . . Adults have a deep psychological need to be generally self-directing, although they may be dependent in particular temporary situations.

Particularly in an online learning environment, adult learners tend, at least early on, to want very clear, specific instructions as to what they are supposed to do and how it is to be done. In effect, they want to produce, or do, what is required.

Over time, however, adult learners tend to become more independent, particularly after they experience some success. Wlodkowski (1984) supports this notion:

> Competence is the concept or major motivation factor that describes our innate desire to take the initiative and effectively act upon our environment rather than remaining passive and allowing the environment to control and determine our behavior.

Still, experience generally shows that despite some periods of uncertainty and dependence, adult learners respond much better when they take some control over their own learning process, and the online environment is very conducive in allowing them some autonomy in their learning.

The characteristics of the learners must always be addressed before instruction is designed. The ASSIST-Me model considers the analysis of learner characteristics as a key step in the design process, indicating that effective, good instruction needs to focus on learners. Failure to consider learner characteristics can lead to poorly designed online instruction that fails to meet the needs of anyone.

However, the individualized nature of distance learning does not mean that interaction with other students is sacrificed. Interaction is often considered an essential element for effective online learning. The ability to work in small groups, in person or in a virtual environment, can result in a more rewarding experience for the students involved. However, according to Kearsley (2000), learners from lower socioeconomic backgrounds are more likely to benefit from more structured activities. Completion of online projects in a collaborative environment can be beneficial for all students. In fact, Simonson et al. (2003) conclude that "[f]ocusing on building collaboration and group interaction may be more important than focusing on individual participation."

ATTITUDES OF LEARNERS

Another key element that needs to be addressed is the attitude of the learners with regard to distance education. Simonson et al. (2003) state that "distance education learners generally have a more favorable attitude toward distance education than do tradition learners, and distance learners feel they learn as well as if they were in a regular classroom." The fact that it is more convenient for many learners, and the ability to have some level of autonomy in their learning process, no doubt contribute to this attitude. Students who have a positive attitude toward learning tend to take it more seriously and, as a result, tend to succeed.

THE ONLINE INSTRUCTOR

The other key participant in any learning situation is the faculty member in charge of delivering instruction. In all models of learning, faculty members are in charge of content and its distribution. Distance learning offices often assist in the process of developing a course for distance delivery to ensure a fit with the technology and with the delivery infrastructure. The instructional design process focuses on determining the goals and expected outcomes of the educational experiences and then matching those goals to the desired instructional strategies and to the supported media (Boettcher & Conrad, 1997).

Compora (2003), however, indicates that some faculty members may not be fully prepared to move into a distance-learning environment:

> Instructors generally teach distance education courses based on their willingness rather than their expertise. The most developed and longest running distance education programs surveyed provide support for both faculty members and students. Faculty members often need help getting started when teaching a course in a different manner than which they are accustomed. Unfortunately, most of the programs surveyed provide little or no training of instructors.

As a result, as technologies and needs change, faculty may require additional training periodically—not just in the planning stages. This is no easy task.

Faculty may perceive obstacles and need to see some measure of reward for adapting their teaching style. A 1999 study pointed out some incentives that make online instruction attractive to faculty members:

> The primary incentives that encourage faculty to adapt their teaching strategies to deliver education via distance center on intrinsic or personal rewards. These include the opportunity to provide innovative instruction and apply new teaching techniques as well as self gratification, fulfilling a personal desire to teach, recognition of their work, and peer recognition. Extending educational opportunities beyond the traditional walls of the institution so

place-bound students have access and students can reduce travel time is also an incentive. Release time for preparation also is a motivator for faculty to teach via distance. (Rockwell, Schauer, Fritz, & Marx, 1999)

Clearly, not only do students see the benefits of online learning, but there are sufficient motivators for faculty members also.

Despite the incentives stated above, there are indeed obstacles, real or perceived, that faculty members see as barriers to teaching in an online environment: "The major perceived obstacles relate to time requirements, developing effective technology skills, and assistance and support needs. Monetary awards for faculty and the cost to the student were seen as neither an incentive nor an obstacle" (Rockwell et al., 1999).

Getting faculty involved is just part of the challenge; keeping them involved and ready to adapt to new technologies as they become available is also a key administrative concern. This is not to say that faculty members are not willing to enter into distance education. Clearly, faculty members are willing to become involved as long as the incentives outweigh the real or perceived obstacles.

To design effective online instruction that will meet the needs of students, faculty members need to determine:

- What content will be covered?
- What are the course (and program) objectives?
- What is the most appropriate way to transmit course material?
- What types of assignments will be required?
- How will tests be administered?
- What textbooks and materials will be required?
- What grading system will be employed?

Faculty members, even those who do not teach distance education courses, possess content expertise and knowledge of the institution's programs, making them a key component in establishing learning outcomes and objectives.

Content is not the only concern, though. Instructors may need to adjust some of their teaching strategies in order to meet the needs of the students. Faculty members need to design instruction that promotes interaction among students and provides consistent and regular feedback. Faculty may not be aware of the impact their separation from the student has on student perceptions. Kearsley (2000) relates that one of the most common complaints is the lack of timely feedback from their instructors; even just an acknowledgment that the work was received has an impact on student perception. Willis (1994) believes that simply including a student's name in feedback personalizes the instruction and validates the student's efforts. Consistent and timely feedback is important in every learning environment, but in a distance-learning situation, the continued separation between the instructor and the learner makes it even more important.

THE NEED TO FOLLOW A MODEL

One of the greatest concerns regarding the design of online instruction is the fact that in order to compete and meet the needs of students, many institutions are being forced into distance education. The implications of this are far reaching and raise concerns that programs and courses are being implemented without following an established system design process. Stenerson (1998) clearly identifies this problem and its implications:

> Many traditional colleges and universities have been forced to embrace distance education as a result of changing demographics of the student population. Part of the change is the student's access to efficient and relevant information. In turn, they are requiring educational institutions to apply efficient information access to academic programs and courses. The information technology exists for this application providing for computer-based instruction or asynchronous learning networks. These provisions are creating the "virtual campus." Many institutions have overlooked, or are not aware of, the dimensions of this new classroom.

Stenerson is certainly correct in suggesting that institutions establish a model based on their own situations. However, the ASSIST-Me model is flexible and detailed enough to address most, if not all, instructional needs.

Moore (1989) supports the importance of following a model when he states that "distance education requires planning, development, production, and distribution on a larger scale than is familiar to most teachers and administrators" (cited in Willis, 1994). This lack of familiarity leads to poorly designed and poorly incorporated instruction. Too often, online courses are offered simply because they are convenient and the technology is already in place. Faculty members are often chosen to teach online courses simply because they are willing to teach them—not because they have the necessary background and training. Course content is often simply transmitted in a different way, without considering other elements the new medium allows. In effect, educators are placing old wine in new wineskins and failing to reap the benefits of the new product.

Therefore, it is imperative that course and lesson designs meet the needs of the students. Content objectives need to be the determining factor in choosing an instructional delivery method. Too often, the delivery method is chosen before the course content is even determined. According to Dabbagh and Bannan-Ritland (2005), "The creation process for online course content is often perceived to be the direct transfer or copying of traditional curricular material to the Web with little or no modification. Simply transferring a course that is taught onsite and offering it via distance education delivery system is nearly impossible. Cotton (1997) presents data regarding higher education spending on distance education:

> Seventy-seven percent of all course sections are taught using courses that are either specifically designed for distance learning, or hybrid courses which are designed for either distance or on site. Only the remaining 23 percent of distance learning courses are really identical to on-site courses which have been "stretched" to accommodate distance learning delivery.

Clearly, this data shows that distance education requires more than just transmitting the instruction in a different way. Content objectives need to be clear because extensive planning, development, and revision of instructional materials is often required in order to meet the needs of students.

OBJECTIVES

Educational objectives make it clear what the students are to learn. Effective objectives are essential to successful utilization of the ASSIST-Me model. Heinich, Molenda, Russell, and Smaldino (1996) present four components that need to be addressed while developing objectives:

Audience: Effective objectives focus on what the learner is doing, not what the instructor is doing.

Behavior: This should be an observable action that indicates whether or not the learner has successfully learned the material (i.e., explain, identify, design, define).

Conditions: Specifies the conditions under which the performance is to be observed.

Degree: This should state what degree of accuracy or proficiency the learners must show. Also, the criterion that will be used to judge the performance must be made clear.

Objectives are the major goals of the instruction. With clearly stated objectives, learners know what the desired outcomes are, the conditions under which they must be able to perform the required behaviors, and how well they must perform them. Objectives are necessary for both the instructor and the learner in order to guide the instructional process. Instructors need to clearly articulate the goal of the instruction so the learners can fulfill them. Trying to teach and learn without a clear goal is like trying to build a house without a blueprint. An effective blueprint considers the key elements before a costly project is undertaken. Similarly, objectives serve as a blueprint for instruction; if followed, effective instruction and learning are more likely to take place.

Specific criteria need to be established by which courses are selected and materials are developed for distance delivery. Dick and Reiser (1989) state:

When instruction is systematically developed, the course has organization, logical consistency, and wholeness that can engage students and supply the conditions for efficient learning. . . . The first step of defining the constraints of budgets, time until delivery, and technical specifications of the delivery system must be taken into account . . . a formal design process for the instruction should be undertaken: writing objective, developing criterion test items, structuring content into hierarchies, and selecting appropriate media forms.

Depending on the content, some courses, such as seminar courses, do not lend themselves as well to distance education delivery methods. With course content that is more abstract, more group discussion is needed. Teaching a seminar course via the Internet would not likely be the best option. Therefore, directors of these programs must develop criteria based on needs assessment, determining which courses are best taught traditionally, on television, or on the World Wide Web.

Once content issues are decided, it is important for planners to determine which delivery method will be used to deliver the instruction. Steiner (1995) supports the notion that the instructional delivery method should be chosen based on the instructional goals:

When choosing a distance education mode, first ask what is your educational need or goal? You must look at each technology and think about how it might fit your teaching goals. . . . Then, you must assess the characteristics and needs of the learning audience. Do not get bogged down by one technology.

This goal-centered approach can allow institutions to make use of existing technologies while being open to new ones; this approach can help maintain cost effectiveness while meeting the needs of students. The ASSIST-Me model does place the needs of the student ahead of the available technologies.

As for the future of distance education in the United States, three major factors indicate a trend toward further growth and involvement among higher education institutions:

1. Institutions are looking to increase enrollment by attracting non-resident students;
2. There are growing needs of adult learners to acquire new skills and college credits while overcoming the constraints of time and distance; and
3. The development of new technologies are making the delivery of distance learning courses more attractive. (Aoki & Pogroszewski, 1998)

The ways in which instruction is delivered to students has undergone profound changes throughout the century. Instructors must be ready to adapt to these changes in order to meet the ever-changing needs of the students.

SUMMARY

Technology has made distance education attractive to both students and administration, and this trend is likely to continue into the twenty-first century as the technology used to deliver instruction continues to evolve. Understanding the needs of the learner is a fundamental instructional design concept. Like the technologies involved in online learning, the students themselves are also an ever-changing, dynamic population.

One key administrative concern is getting faculty involved and ready to adapt to new technologies as they become available. Faculty members may perceive various obstacles to teaching in an online environment and may require additional training or support. Clearly, faculty members are willing to become involved as long as support is available and the incentives outweigh the obstacles.

The ASSIST-Me model seeks to ensure that online instruction is carefully developed and implemented, and that online courses are included into curricula only following a well-thought-out process. These steps are required to help ensure that distance education programs and online instruction fit the ever-changing needs of the students while remaining effective and efficient.

REFERENCES

Aoki, K., & Pogroszewski, D. (1998, Fall). Virtual university reference model: A guide to delivering education and support services to the distance learner. *Online journal of distance learning administration*, *1*(3). Accessed December 13, 2004, from http://www.westga.edu/~distance/aoki13.html.

Boettcher, J., & Conrad, R. (1997, June). Distance learning: A faculty FAQ. *Syllabus 10* (10), 14–17, 54.

Compora, D. (2003). Current trends in distance education: An administrative model. *Online journal of distance learning*, *6*(2). Accessed December 16, 2004, from http://www.westga.edu/%7Edistance/ojdla/summer62/compora62.html.

Cotton, C. (1997, October). Administrators plan for distance learning: Examining higher education spending trends. *Syllabus*, *11*(3), 50–51.

Dabbagh, N., & Bannan Ritland, B. (2005). *Online learning: concepts, strategies, and application*. Upper Saddle River, NJ: Pearson/Merrill/Prentice Hall.

Dick, W., & Reiser, R. (1989). *Planning effective instruction*. Englewood Cliffs, NJ: Prentice Hall.

Downes, S. (1998, Fall). The future of online learning. *Online journal of distance learning administration*, *1*(3). Accessed December 16, 2004, from http://www.westga.edu/~distance/downes13.html.

Gustafson, K., & Branch, R. (2002). What is instructional design? In R. Reiser & J. Dempsey (Eds.), *Trends and issues in instructional design and technology* (pp. 16–25). Upper Saddle River, NJ: Pearson.

Heinich, R., Molenda, M., Russell, J., & Smaldino, S. (1996). *Instructional media and technologies for learning*. (5th ed.). Englewood Cliffs, NJ: Merrill.

Kearsley, G. (2000). *Online education: Learning and teaching in cyberspace*. Stamford, CT: Wadsworth Thomson Learning.

Knowles, M. (1980). *The modern practice of adult education: From pedagogy to andragogy*. Chicago: Follett.

Minton, T., & Willet, L. (2003). Student preferences for academic structure and content in a distance education setting. *Online journal of distance learning*, *6*(1). Accessed December 2, 2004, from http://www.westga.edu/%7Edistance/ojdla/spring61/minton61.htm.

Moore, M., & Kearsley, G. (1996). *Distance education: A systems view*. Belmont, CA: Wadsworth.

Rockwell, S., Schauer, J., Fritz, S., & Marx, D. (1999, Winter). Incentives and obstacles influencing higher education faculty and administrators to teach via distance. *Online journal of distance learning administration*, *2*(4). Accessed December 12, 2004, from http://www.westga.edu/~distance/rockwell24.html.

Simonson, M., Smaldino, S., Albright, M., & Zvacek, S. (2003). *Teaching and learning at a distance: Foundations of distance education*, (2nd ed.). Upper Saddle River, NJ: Merrill/Prentice Hall.

Steiner, V. (1995, October). *What is distance education?* Accessed May 8, 2000, from http://www.wested.org/tie/dlrn/distance.html.

Stenerson, J. (1998). Systems analysis and design for a successful distance education program implementation. *Online journal of distance learning administration, 1*(2). Accessed December 9, 2004, from http://www.westga.edu/~distance/Stener12.html.

Thompson, M. (1998). Distance learners in higher education. In C. C. Gibson (Ed.), *Distance learners in higher education* (pp. 9–24). Madison, WI: Atwood.

Willis, B. (Ed.). (1994). *Distance education: strategies and tools.* Englewood Cliffs, NJ: Educational Technology Publications.

Wlodkowski, R. J. (1984). *Enhancing adult motivation to learn: A guide to improving instruction and increasing learner achievement.* San Francisco: Jossey-Bass.

Part 2

THE ASSIST-ME MODEL FOR WEB-BASED INSTRUCTION

INTRODUCTION TO THE ASSIST-ME MODEL FOR WEB-BASED INSTRUCTION

This online design model flows from the first step to the last step and is simple to follow. The key to this model is to proceed through each step of the design in an orderly way. The model consists of seven basic steps, each having substeps to consider:

Step 1: Analyze Instruction, Curriculum, Instructional Setting, and Students

Step 2: State Performance Objectives

Step 3: Select Instructional Materials, Organization of Content, and Media

Step 4: Implement Instruction, Extended Syllabus, Modules, and Orientation

Step 5: Solicit Student Response to Instruction

Step 6: Test, Evaluate, and Revise Instruction

Step 7: Maintenance of an Online Course

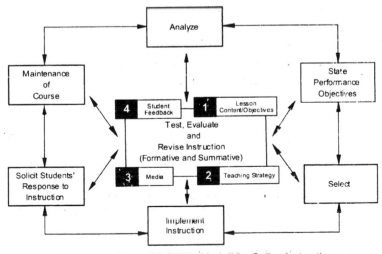

Core Model: The "ASSIST-Me Model" for Online Instruction

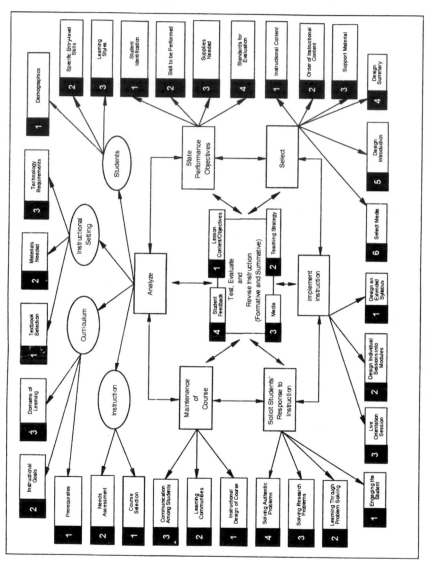

The "ASSIST-Me Model" for Online Instruction

You will notice each step is grouped into segments with arrows pointing to what is to be designed in each of these areas. You will also note that in the core of the ASSIST-Me model, arrows run from each step. marked Test, Evaluate, and Revise Instruction, to the center of the model and back to the step being designed. Throughout the design phase, you should be constantly evaluating your design procedure, using the formative evaluation process detailed in step 6. When the last phase of the design has been completed in step 5, and at the end of the course, the entire course should be evaluated using the summative process. also detailed in step 6.

BLENDED COURSES

Teaching in the traditional classroom to teaching an online course represents a radical departure. A gradual approach may be used to ultimately teach a complete online course. For those who do not wish to make the radical change from the classroom to total online teaching, a blended approach may be used.

Level 1	Traditional	Course with no online technology used.
		Content is communicated orally and in writing.
		Students attend class as usual.
		Students participate in lectures and discussions.
Level 2	Web-facilitated	Course uses Web to post syllabus, assignments, etc.
		May use e-mail for course announcements, etc.
Level 3	Blended	Substantial portion of content is delivered online.
		Discussions are held online.
		There is a limited amount of the traditional face-to-face classes.
Level 4	Online	Entire course is conducted online.
		No face to face classes.

USE OF CONSTRUCTIVISM AS AN ONLINE TEACHING STYLE

Although a specific style has not been indicated to use as an online teaching, it is strongly recommended that the constructivist approach, or a similar approach, be considered (see chapter 2). This style purports the engagements of students in authentic and meaningful learning experiences. It suggests that students, given an opportunity to learn a new concept, theory, principle, and so on, work together as a team to construct their own knowledge, a process to obtain their solution, and be able to interpret their findings for their own understanding. This style promotes various ways students may assemble knowledge and use this knowledge to facilitate thinking and problem solving in real-life situations.

CHAPTER 4

Step 1: Analyze Instruction, Settings, and Students

KNOWLEDGE OBJECTIVES

At the end of this chapter, you should be able to:

1. List the selection criteria for an online course.
2. Define course goals and give an example.
3. Describe the purpose of a needs assessment and when it should be administered.
4. Describe the practical issues of the instructional setting.
5. List the characteristics of student demographics when analyzing distance-learning students.
6. Explain why the verification of entry-level skills is important to the design process.
7. Describe the importance of learning styles to the instructional design process.
8. Describe the way in which learning styles influence the way in which the WBI is designed

(continued)

(continued)

9. Explain the differences in learning styles and give examples.
10. Define perceptual preferences and strengths.
11. Describe the four information-processing behaviors.
12. Explain how motivational factors influence student learning.
13. Describe how psychological behaviors can create a negative effect on learning.

LEXICON

Terms to know:

abstract random	entry-level skills
abstract sequential	kinesthetic learning
affective domain	learning styles
cognitive domain	motor skill domain
cognitive strategies	needs assessment
concrete random	SKA
concrete sequential	student demographics
domains of learning	visual learning

Several faculty members were faced with the daunting task of developing an updated version of a computer class that would satisfy all of the International Society for Technology in Education (ISTE) standards, state standards, as well as standards that had been developed by the national organization. After several months of designing the instruction and multiple drafts, the faculty finalized the curriculum for this course that would satisfy all requirements as well as all of the state licensure requirements. The required text for this course was carefully selected using criteria that would satisfy all standards as well as making the course as interesting, challenging, and as practical as possible.

The course started in the fall with 14 sections having 25 students in each section. Five faculty were assigned to teach these sections. As the fall semester progressed, the faculty began to notice there was an extremely high rate of absenteeism and failure to complete assignments on time in each of the sections. Often students were not in attendance when there was free computer time to complete assignments and missed the laboratory assignments when demonstration and instruction was given for the next assignment.

The faculty spent many hours assessing the problem and quickly agreed to develop and administer a survey that would obtain information as to the computer skill level of the students as well as their attitudes toward the course.

After the survey was administered and the data collected, the faculty members were dismayed to learn that most of the students had already learned the basic computer skills being taught in previous courses, either in high school or in other college courses. The survey disclosed, however, that advanced word-processing skills as well as basic to advanced Excel practices needed to be taught. The survey also revealed that the students had a very negative attitude toward the assignments and the way the course was being taught. The students were not being challenged in their assignments and thought the assignments were elementary and not applicable to their situations. The students indicated that they did not want to come to class because it was a waste of time and that they really did not care whether or not they completed the assignments.

This situation is a classic example of designing instruction without conducting the proper analysis of the instruction, instructional setting, and especially student analysis. If the students had been surveyed before taking this course, the faculty would have been able to design instruction that would teach the students what they *did not know*. The faculty had made a faulty assessment, assuming that since this was a required course, the students did not have any of the necessary computer skills.

ANALYZE INSTRUCTION

Analysis for Course Selection

Before you set the pen to paper or turn on your computer to begin designing sessions for your WBI, several concerns need to be considered and addressed before analyzing the instruction, setting, or students. Generally, faculty and designers omit this step, making the assumption that any course that is taught in the classroom is suitable to be taught on the Web. However, consideration must be given to the environment that has changed for WBI. The teacher and student are now geographically separated by time and space, reducing the rapid feedback to questions concerning course content, assignments, and testing experienced in the classroom setting. Required facilities and resources also need to be considered. What is needed is an analysis for the course online selection criteria that would include: (1) the number of students who may take the course, (2) whether the course is required or an elective, (3) the type of course content to be taught, (4) the level of the course, and (5) student attitudes.

The number of students who may take this course is of prime consideration in the selection process. This same consideration is made for an instructional television series. In both cases, a student-driven model is used. Creating a course for only a few students is a waste of resources, time, and energy. The return on investment (ROI), which educators are generally not concerned about but found in business, is an important consideration. ROI simply means that the number of hours and resources it takes to design the course will be offset by the number of students who enroll to take the course. It takes many more hours and resources to design a course for the Web than it would for the classroom. If the analysis of the student population discloses that an adequate number of students will enroll in this course on a regular basis, the course can be considered for WBI.

Whether the course is required or elective must also be considered. To some extent, this is an extension of the first requirement: a student population large enough to justify the online course. If the course is a required course and the student population is large enough within the department, then the course can be easily justified. If, however, the course is an elective within the curriculum, a careful analysis of previous course enrollment must be performed. Trends of student enrollment in a course can change over a few years or even in a few semesters. A decline in student population available for the course will also impact the course selection.

Course content must also be evaluated. Hard sciences, social sciences, theory, and philosophy courses each have a dramatically different type of content and range from concrete information, as in the sciences, to very abstract information in philosophy courses. The hard sciences such as mathematics, biology, and chemistry—sometimes referred to as concrete courses—generally require less exchange of ideas than do philosophy courses, which are extremely abstract and require an extensive exchange of ideas for purposes of clarification and concept building. The more abstract a course becomes, the greater the requirement for communication and the exchange of ideas, concepts, and theory for students to clarify their own ideas, concepts, and theories.

The next criterion to consider is the level of the course to be taught. Lower-division courses, in which students learn the fundamentals of a given discipline, tend to be more concrete. However, lower-level students may have more of a difficult time adjusting to a course that is taught by a teacher who is not present. They also may have problems with delayed feedback and the additional responsibility of independent learning. As students progress in their field of study, courses tend to become more abstract as various theories are introduced. In graduate-level courses, there is a preponderance of theory, since graduate-level courses are built on previously learned concepts. Logically, as we discussed in the previous section, more student discussion is required as the course content becomes more abstract. It must be determined if the type of class interaction is appropriate for WBI, especially in seminar courses where there is ample student participation.

An additional consideration is the attitude among the students at various educational levels. Undergraduate students, especially at the lower levels, are experiencing for the first time in their education a certain amount of freedom in their course selection, the time the course will meet, the instructor for the course, and the amount of time spent preparing for each class and preparing for examinations. Responsible students find this to be a rewarding challenge, while the less responsible students may find this to be difficult in time management and preparation. For some students whose academic *lightbulb* has not yet been turned on, the notion of having an online course creates an emotional feeling of abandonment. Students may find themselves disorganized and confused. For the most part, undergraduate students are trying to learn how to learn. Graduate-level students, however, have a different attitude toward learning. They tend to be highly motivated, independent, and responsible, since they have elected to work on an advanced degree and are now paying more for their education than they did as undergraduates. Class and assignment preparation usually is more thorough, more class participation is exhibited, and greater care is taken in the completion of class assignments and taking examinations. Depending upon the graduate program, there may be major and minor exams over all the course material taken by graduate students that increases their motivation to learn course content. Graduate students have the incentives to spend time learning course content and to earn the graduate degree.

Analyze Needs Assessment

Once the decision has been made to select a specific course to be developed for WBI, a decision must be made as to whether to administer a needs assessment. Most instructional design models suggest that a needs assessment be conducted to determine what the students know and what the students do not know. This is commonly referred to as a gap: the disparity of knowledge, or the absence of information. Business and industry designers use this technique to discover if employees have the necessary prerequisite knowledge. If they have the knowledge and/or skill, the designer will omit the training. In education, however, it may be taken as a given if a course is contained in a program curriculum that students do not have all of the necessary extensive cognitive formal knowledge. However, it should not be overlooked that at least some students may have already learned some of the course content. Caution should be exercised if a needs assessment will not be conducted. A careful review of previously taken courses will be helpful in assessing the knowledge and skill levels. A helpful guideline to follow is that if in doubt of a student's prior knowledge and skill level, it would be prudent to administer a needs assessment.

ANALYZE THE CURRICULUM

Analyze Course Prerequisites

We are familiar with two basic types of courses found in the curriculum: entry-level courses and courses that require prerequisite knowledge. Entry-level courses are generally those courses that are introductory courses and are taken first. These courses may not require an extensive prior knowledge in the field of study but require general knowledge skills of reading, vocabulary, and writing. If, however, the course requires prerequisite knowledge, then the entry-level skills evaluation should be conducted, even if students have taken the prerequisite courses, to determine if any gaps in knowledge are present. At this time, you may want to administer some type of needs assessment to determine exactly what skills the students have or do not have. For example, if a student is pursuing the study of measurement, the introductory course in statistics has no course prerequisites. However, if the student is taking a course in research design, he or she probably will be required to have taken Statistics I and II courses.

Analyze Instructional Goals

One of the primary steps in the design process is to determine the instructional goals for the course. These course goals are the general and very broad statements of what the students will be able to do or perform by the end of the instruction. These learning goals (Smith & Ragan, 1999) describe "what ought to be." This list directs you to focus on what students are to learn in the course. For example, in an educational technology course, one of the goals for the course could be that students will be able to properly select and integrate various forms of mediated instruction that will reinforce the performance objectives.

When designing these goals, you probably will also want to determine the existence of national goal standards, state standards, professional standards, or school standards for your course. If applicable, these standards need to be included in your goal statements.

Analyze Domains of Learning

Once course goals have been identified, you need to determine the type or combination of the types of learning that will occur. In his *Taxonomy of Educational Objectives*, Bloom (1956) created types or domains of learning. He recognized there was more than one type or combination of types of learning and created the categories of *cognitive* for mental skills (knowledge), *affective* for growth in feelings skills (attitude), and *psychomotor* for the manual or physical skills (skills). These are also referred to as knowledge, attitude, and skills. Teachers often refer to these as KAS, SKA, or KSA.

The cognitive domain involves the acquisition of knowledge and intellectual skills. This domain would include the recall of specific facts, procedures, and concepts that serve in the development of intellectual abilities and skills. This type of learning may also be referred to as declarative knowledge, that the student knows something very specific (Gagné, 1985). The students have learned this knowledge by memorizing facts or concepts but are not required to apply this knowledge. For example, students may be required to list all 50 states, but that does not mean that they could find them on a map or describe specific characteristics. Intellectual skills are different than declarative knowledge in that students must apply knowledge they have learned to a different situation. In the case of memorizing all 50 states, the student might be required to locate the states that will be affected by a large storm front.

The affective domain refers to how or the manner in which we manage events emotionally, such as feelings, values, appreciation, motivations, and attitudes. Attitudes reflect the choices we make from the stimulus, for example, how we react to having to take a course we do not like, such as chemistry, physics, or algebra. In this case, the student probably does not like math and wants to avoid these courses. Attitudes can easily be shaped by what is broadcast on television or seen in movie theatres. For example, films on World War II, such as *Band of Brothers* or *Saving Private Ryan*, will shape your feelings about the brutality of battle, sacrifices made by individual soldiers, or conduct by high-ranking officers, helping to shape your attitudes toward the event.

The third domain of learning, psychomotor skills, deals with the muscular movements of the body. Gross bodily movements are found in sports of every kind, such as football, basketball, and baseball, as well as golf, swimming, running, and so on. These sports can be learned by watching a role model and then by having a coach give you direct instruction as to your muscular motion. Fine motor skills, such as painting a portrait, drawing a still life, singing, playing a musical instrument, or even typing on a computer keyboard, fall into this category. Although these motor skills are visible and can be observed, they are also dependent upon a cognitive component, usually a procedural rule that organizes the kind of sequence of actions.

ANALYZE THE INSTRUCTIONAL SETTING

This stage of instructional analysis deals with some very practical issues. First, the selection of the textbook for the course to be developed is of crucial importance. Multiple texts are available and must meet very specific criteria within the department. Criteria may include:

- compatibility with the curriculum;
- the accuracy and currency of the content;
- motivation of students;
- availability of an instructor manual; and
- clarity of organization

The second consideration is additional material students may need for the course, for example, a workbook or a calculator, detailed instruction of the use of a Web site, and so on. Third, a general knowledge of the technology requirements used to deliver the instruction is required, which includes an explanation of the use of WebCT, Blackboard, or other delivery systems. You will also want to inform the students of all computer requirements before they enroll in the course.

ANALYZE THE STUDENTS

The much-overlooked analysis is that of the students who will be enrolled in the course. Little or no time is generally spent reviewing and gathering this data. This being the case, you may be very apt not to design course content that will meet the students' level of knowledge, skills, and attitude (KSAs). The more you know about the target audience, the better your instruction will be designed. When designing your instruction, it is extremely critical that it be designed for a particular student group, rather than designing the instruction around the content and then search for a student group. Therefore, you should generally consider three basic categories of the learner: student demographics, specific entry-level skills, and learning styles.

Student Demographics

The analysis of student demographics may be the easiest to perform. These characteristics include: age, gender, level of education, ethnicity, and socioeconomic background. Age is important when considering the maturity of the student. Generally, the older the student, the more developed the cognitive strategies. Conversely, the younger the student, the less developed the cognitive strategies. If you are designing an online course for high school students, age becomes more important in regard to the development of the way the students process the information. If you are designing a course for college students, the maturity level is higher; college students tend to have better learning skills. If you are designing instruction for a graduate-level course, at either the master's or doctoral level, age is not necessarily an important factor. For the most part, graduate-level students have elected to pursue a graduate degree on a voluntary basis to further their career goals. Learning content becomes paramount in their studies. Graduate students study to learn course content.

Gender is generally important at the lower educational levels, such as in high school. When college or graduate-level courses are designed, the differences in the way the genders learn are greatly reduced.

The students' academic background and level of education need to be addressed. Generally, a college student may take any college course unless specific level requirements are in place; for example, sophomore level, junior standing, and the like, or prerequisite requirements. Likewise, for graduate courses there may be some that may be taken at any time when the course becomes available unless prerequisites are required.

Ethnicity may also be considered. One should be cautious as to why these factors may be considered. However, this factor is considered because various racial groups may have common experiences due to their groups' membership that might be different from those of members of other groups.

Finally, the socioeconomic background of a student is important for high school and lower-level college students. If you were to take a student from a very wealthy family who lives in an upper-class neighborhood, chances are the parents are well educated. The parents can offer their child educational benefits that enhance his or her learning. The parents are also a primary factor in initially teaching their child many basics, such as speaking skills, grammar, use of numbers, and so on. Contrast this background with a student who is from the inner city whose parents (or parent) may or may not be high school graduates. Their educational background is extremely limited and they may not be able or know how to teach their child any of the fundamentals. You will notice a vast difference in entry-level skills as well as learning ability. Therefore, it is extremely important that the socioeconomic background be explored when designing the instruction.

Specific Entry-Level Skills

Often, the instructor judges that students who enroll in their class do not possess knowledge of the subject content (Morrison, Ross, & Kemp, 2004). The course has been carefully designed as part of the curriculum and students need this information to proceed further in their field of study. The instructor must judge that the students have the skills to process and comprehend this new information.

This analysis is not often entirely correct. True, some students may not have extensive and specific knowledge of the subject content, but they often have at least some prerequisite knowledge. Recall the example used in the introduction to this chapter. The instructional design faculty failed to conduct a needs assessment to identify the computer skills the students had already learned. The result was poor student performance as well as poor attendance. Failure to initially administer this needs assessment caused the faculty to spend additional time revising their instruction, and students developed a negative attitude toward the course.

This example illustrates the need to verify entry-level skills. This may be done formally at the beginning of the course by administering a pretest, or informally by administering some type of survey or interview that obtains information as to the skills, knowledge, and attitude already possessed by the students. Verification of the entry-level skills, however, may not have to be performed every time the same course is offered. The data collected during several semesters may be kept and then, by a comparative analysis, used to determine the level at which the course should be designed.

Some specific entry-level skills should be required for the course. In addition to the traditional skills of reading, comprehension, vocabulary, and problem-solving skills, there may be specific skills the students need. If you are teaching an entry-level computer literacy course, the prerequisite skills students must have need to be clearly stated. In this case, the students must have basic keyboarding skills, a basic knowledge of the operating system for the computer, and basic skills for operating the computer. These skills should be stated in performance objective form in the course description and in the course syllabus (more on this in chapter 7). In addition, research reveals that students' prior knowledge of a particular subject influences how and what they learn in the new course (Dick, Carey, & Carey, 2001). The greater the prior knowledge, the more the students will probably learn in the new course. This research also impacts how you design your instruction as well. If students have some prior knowledge of the subject content, a more unstructured approach may be used along with more group discussions and open-ended questions. If students do not have any background in the subject, it may be much better to use a well-organized and structured approach.

Learning Styles

Learning style refers to a group of psychological traits that determine how a student perceives, interacts, and responds to the subject content and learning environment (Smaldino et al., 2005). For the most part, you are probably unaware that the way you design your content is the way you learn. Each of us has our own way in which we learn cognitive material and motor skills. Each of us has developed our own way of learning, and we use what works best for us. However, our own unique learning style may not be the way our students learn.

The literature on learning styles emphasizes that the vast majority of faculty who design instruction design the way they themselves learn. To the instructor, this is an acceptable way to design instruction. However, this procedure completely overlooks the learning styles of the majority of students.

A great number of formal learning style inventories have been developed in recent years, and the reliability of these inventories is quite high. Dunn and Dunn (1992) developed an instrument that measures the variance in learning styles. Many instruments also identify a backup learning style if the primary learning style does not work with either the subject content or the way the instruction has been designed.

Here is an informal learning style inventory (Koontz, 1996) that has been successfully used in many classes by the author and has reinforced the research finding that nearly every student in your class will have a similar to a vastly different learning style. Try this first on yourself and then administer it to your students. Then make a comparison of the variety of ways we learn.

Determine how you study to learn by underlining those items that best describe your learning behavior.

1. *Environment*, e.g., need silence *or* a radio in the background; bright *or* dim lighting; cool, moderate, *or* warm temperature; an informal setting with a lounge chair, coach, bed, *or* a formal setting with a hard chair, library table or desk, etc.
2. *Emotional elements*, e.g., motivated, persistent, responsible, *or* unmotivated, not persistent, irresponsible, etc.
3. *Structure*, e.g., independent, need little *or* no guidance, can follow directions easily, can comprehend objectives, minimum amount of feedback on progress, *or* dependent on instructor for guidance, need objectives explained, need feedback
4. *Sociological elements*, e.g., prefer to work alone, work with a peer, *or* work with a large group, work with a trainer, *or* some combination
5. *Physical elements*, e.g., prefer early morning, *or* afternoon, *or* evening classes; need to eat or nibble on something *or* cannot eat anything; need to move around *or* can sit constantly still; can study for long periods of time (1–3 hours) *or* need frequent breaks
6. *Classroom instructional elements,* e.g., visual learner using print, mediated instruction, including overhead transparencies, television, etc.; *or* auditory learner, i.e., just listening to a teacher or class discussion to gain information; *or* a combination of visual and auditory learner
7. *Response elements*, e.g., need to be enactive, i.e., actively engaged in learning activity, *or* can learn by abstraction, i.e., reading about subject matter and discussing it
8. *Cognitive strategies are used*, e.g., orally rehearse material to be learned, i.e., repeat items or write items on paper, *or* rehearse material mentally that is to be learned; use associations *or* do not use associations, i.e., just memorize material as required; use mnemonic devices *or* do not use mnemonic devices (ASSIST-Me model is a mnemonic device)

After having the class complete this informal learning inventory, review each category and ask your students to indicate their learning style. When finished, conduct a class discussion and have your students summarize what they have learned about learning styles. Students should recognize that no two students have exactly the same learning style. Therefore, you can conclude from this very informal learning style exercise that when designing instruction, a variety of teaching strategies must be used that will accommodate various learning styles.

Learning styles, as described in the literature, can be categorized into perceptual preferences and strengths, information-processing traits, motivational factors, and psychological traits (Smaldino et al., 2005).

Perceptual Preferences and Strengths

Learners will have various preferences as to which sensory gateways they prefer to use. The main gateways include auditory, visual, tactile, and kinesthetic. When students are asked to identify their own perceptual preference or strengths, they generally do not realize they prefer to learn visually. They immediately think visual learning is from television, the computer screen, or a PowerPoint lesson. They are correct. However, they do not consider the visual learning that takes place when reading assignments in their textbook. According to the literature (Gagné, 1985), approximately 85% of students are visual learners and approximately 15% are auditory learners. If this is true, we need to rethink how much value should be placed on the traditional lecture style of delivering content information.

Tactile learning, also called enactive or hands-on learning, is necessary in courses where objects of instruction are studied. For example, in a computer course, the student must manipulate the computer's operating system and software programs to learn the necessary skills. Kinesthetic learning engages both large and fine motor skills. Again, in the computer course, fine motor skills should be learned and mastered in using the keyboard.

These two forms of learning style are also important to use with students who have forms of a learning disability, who tend to prefer tactile and/or kinesthetic learning. These students find it extremely difficult to sit quietly in a chair or desk and read, answer questions, and join in class and group discussions.

Information-Processing Behavior

This type of learning has a range of variables as to how students tend to approach the cognitive processing of information (Butler, 1986). Gregorc's model, as cited in Butler, categorizes learners into concrete versus abstract and random versus sequential. This evolves into four basic categories. First, *concrete sequential* students prefer enactive learning that is structured and in a logical order, that is, the hands-on approach as in using a workbook, drill and practice, and structured demonstrations. Students who are *concrete random* learners work best in an environment of trial-and-error learning, similar to the constructive way of learning, and can obtain conclusions from exploring material. These students prefer games, simulations, independent learning, and discovery learning. *Abstract sequential* learners are adept at decoding verbal and symbolic messages. They prefer reading the textbook assigned for the course as well as outside readings, and listening and processing the cognitive material contained in a lecture. In the last category, *abstract random*, students learn well in using mediated instruction. They can decode messages contained in instructional television lessons or online lessons. They also contribute and do well in group discussions.

Motivational Factors

The range of student motivation that will assist the students in learning in your class will vary from extremely unmotivated students to very highly motivated students. Motivation is emotional and it is the amount of effort the student will invest in learning, the desire to learn, and the degree of attention toward the subject content. Motivation deals with students' real feelings toward themselves, toward other students, toward the course, and toward you as the instructor. The lack of motivation can be so strong that a student will not do well in the class due to his intense dislike for the subject content and/or the instructor.

Motivation is also influenced by the amount of control the students have in the class. If students perceive that they have absolutely no control over any part of the course, motivation to learn may be low. Conversely, if the students realize that they do have some control over the class, for example, the students do not have control over what they learn but do have control over how they learn, motivation tends to be higher. Motivation also deals with how the course is structured, the type of feedback received from the instructor, positive or negative, and the degree of competitiveness and timidity of the student.

A second-semester master's student was enrolled in an upper-level seminar course designed for both master's and doctoral students. In this course, students studied the phenomenon of the psychology of speech.

During the first day of class, the well-seasoned senior professor of the communications department came into the class and sat down at the large mahogany conference table. It just so happened that all the students were male. As the gray-haired professor looked over his half glasses and stared at the students for what seemed to be an usual length of time, he finally exclaimed in a forceful and stern voice, "Gentlemen, you have just spent at least four years learning how to study! In this class, we study to learn! Are there any questions?"

After the shock of this statement began to sink into the students' psyches, they all knew they were taking a course that was going to be exceptionally demanding as well as difficult.

What type of psychological motivational factor did this challenge have on the students' motivation? If the professor was using this as an example of how speech can influence student behavior, then he was very successful. Some students became highly motivated to do well and accepted the challenge of learning. For others, it created a very high level of anxiety and fear of making mistakes.

We can learn much from this example. Creating an atmosphere conducive to learning that will motivate students to perform well is extremely important. Frequent praise and gentle correction are much more effective than harsh criticism and correction that embarrass the student.

Psychological Factors

Psychological factors deal with gender, health conditions, and environmental conditions. Of these factors, health issues, at times, become a dominating factor. Hunger, not feeling well, or impending medical procedures will create a level of anxiety that can interfere with learning. For adult learners, health issues appear to be more important than the time of day the class is offered, the temperature, lighting conditions, or existing noise.

Now that you have explored various learning styles and have learned of the wide variance in the way students learn, you need to apply this to your instructional process. As a result, you will need to use an eclectic or diverse instructional design style that will accommodate the various learning styles. For the concrete sequential students, you will want to use a workbook, some drill-and-practice, or a structured demonstration. At other times, you will want to create assignments for the abstract random students that use a constructionist or trial-and-error learning. Or you may want to assign reading material for the abstract sequential students and then use an audio insert for the WBI that discusses what your students have read. Finally, for the abstract random students, you may want to assign them to view a television segment and decode the information to be learned, followed by a class discussion.

SUMMARY

Not all courses are suitable for Web-based instruction. What is needed is an analysis of the criteria for course selection, which would include:

1. the number of students who may take the course;
2. whether the course is required or an elective;
3. the type of course content to be taught;
4. the level of the course; and
5. student attitudes.

An analysis of course prerequisites will need to be conducted. Even entry-level courses need to be analyzed in terms of the skills students may already possess. A needs assessment may be administered to obtain the necessary information as to the level of knowledge of the students. Declared prerequisite knowledge will also have to be analyzed, in other words, have students taken the necessary prerequisite courses to be admitted into this course? If so, you must determine if gaps in their knowledge exist.

Instructional goals, which are very broad statements identifying what the students must be able to perform by the end of the instruction, will need to be written. After these goals have been outlined, you will need to determine the types or combination of types of learning that will occur. These domains of learning are classified as cognitive for mental skills or knowledge, affective for feeling skills or attitude, and psychomotor skills that represents physical skills.

Practical issues of textbook selection, identification of supplementary materials such as workbooks, and directions as to how to use the delivery system will satisfy the analysis of the instructional setting.

The much-overlooked analysis of students who will enroll in your course will need to be conducted. This would include student demographics, specific entry skills and learning styles. Student demographics include age, gender, level of education, ethnicity, and socioeconomic background. Specific entry-level skills need to be determined by conducting a needs assessment that establishes any gaps in the students' knowledge for your course even if there are no prerequisites. Finally, it is extremely important to understand that each student has his or her own unique learning style. Instruction needs to be designed using an eclectic style that will accommodate the various learning styles.

CASE STUDIES

Course Description No. 1

Course: BIOL 6000/8000 Introduction to Scientific Thought and Expression
Instructor: Dr. Earnest DuBrul, associate professor, biology
Course description: [3 hours] A writing intensive course for new graduate students that focuses on scientific hypothesis testing and reading the original literature in biology. Prerequisites: Although this is an entry-level course for the graduate school, in-service teachers would have had courses both in mathematics and science.

Introduction to Scientific Thought and Expression is a graduate-level elective course for both master's and doctoral students who are science educators. The number of students who elect to take this course ranges from 4–10 students.

Instructional goals:

1. To demonstrate the idea that the universe is understandable to human beings through our senses without recourse to the supernatural entities and that it obeys physical laws.
2. To present science as "one of the grand adventures of exploration characterized by odysseys of pure thought which are often inspired by empirical information."
3. To demonstrate the aesthetic qualities of science and an awareness of those moral and ethical issues that stem from science.
4. To investigate the different ways scientists communicate their ideas and research to other scientists and to the scientific community.

Domains of learning: The domains of learning for this course include both cognitive and affective domains of learning.

(continued)

(*continued*)

Students

1. Demographics: There is a cross section of students who are licensed teachers who are teaching science courses.
2. Specific entry-level skills: These graduate-level students are in-service teachers who have had teaching experience in science education and have a bachelor's degree in science education.
3. Learning styles: Learning styles include primarily visual with auditory reinforcement. Tactile learning is used to complete science experiments.

Information-processing skills: As science educators, the majority of these in-service teachers use concrete sequential processing skills with concrete random processing skills when working with scientific experiments. Abstract sequential processing skills are used for reading textbook assignments. Abstract random processing skills are used when viewing multiple televised segments.

Course Description No. 2

Course: MET 3100 Applied Thermodynamics
Instructor: Dr. Ella Fridman, associate professor, engineering technology
Course description: [4 hours] Basic principles and laws of classical thermodynamics, equations of state, reversibility and entropy applied to processes and cycles for ideal and nonideal substances. Prerequisite: ENGT 3020

This Applied Thermodynamics (MET 3100) course is offered in the College of Engineering, Department of Engineering Technology. An average of 2–8 students take this required core course in distance education. The same course is also offered at the same time in a face-to-face course. This is a junior-level course. The majority of the course content is concrete. Student attitude is positive toward subject content.

Instructional goals:

1. To demonstrate basic principles of thermodynamics and applications of these principles to practical engineering problems.
2. To apply and further develop their calculus-based problem-solving skills.
3. To demonstrate skills in data collection and measurement analysis.

(*continued*)

4. Given software application, to demonstrate computer competence by generating their own programs in computational and design assignments.
5. To demonstrate communication skills by writing laboratory and design reports with an oral presentation.
6. To demonstrate cooperative team-working skills in projects and performance of experiments.

Domains of learning: The domains of learning include cognitive skills to analyze course projects and experiments and psychomotor skills in the demonstration of projects. Additional materials needed for this course are the required equipment for laboratory experiments.

Students

1. Demographics: The majority of students (94%+) are males generally from middle-class families. A very low percentage is minority students.
2. Specific entry-level skills: Students must have the required engineering mathematics skills as well as a background in technical thermodynamics.
3. Learning styles: The majority of students are visual learners with auditory and tactile learning skills. The majority of students are concrete sequential learners with a combination of concrete random, abstract sequential, and abstract random skills as a secondary processing skill.

Course Description No. 3

Course: CIEC 3200 Philosophy and Practice in Early Childhood Education
Instructor: Dr. Bob Cryan, professor, early childhood education
Course description: [3 hours] This course emphasizes the role, attitude, and characteristics of the effective teacher of young children.
Prerequisites:

CIEC 1900 Early Childhood Education Linking Seminar I
CIEC 2900 Early Childhood Education Linking Seminar II
SPED 3220 Atypical Development in Early Childhood
CIEC 3210 Child Behavior and Development

(*continued*)

(continued)

The number of students who take this required course will average between 25 and 30. The type of course content is a combination of more concrete content in the area of child development and more abstract in the area of philosophy. Students have a positive attitude toward the content of the course and the course process.

Instructional goals:

1. To describe the profession of early childhood education by examining relevant issues as they relate to the physical, social, emotional, and intellectual development of children from birth to eight years.
2. To identify the current roles of educators and other caregivers while examining how these roles can be enhanced in order to improve the level of care all children receive, regardless of their culture or socioeconomic background.

Domains of learning: The domain of learning for this course is primarily cognitive with the development of a positive attitude toward early childhood philosophy and practice.

Students

1. Demographics: Students in this course are of junior standing. Ninety percent of the students are female, with 10 percent male. They come from socioeconomic groups of upper-middle class, middle class, and lower class.
2. Specific entry-level skills: Students must have passed Praxis I, have a minimum GPA of 2.7, and complete all prerequisite courses.
3. Learning styles: The majority of students are visual learners reinforced by the auditory learning.

Information processing skills: For this course, the primary way of learning is abstract sequential, that is, decoding verbal and symbolic messages from the textbook and from assigned readings. The secondary way, concrete sequential, is of equal impact.

REFERENCES

Bloom, B. (Ed.). (1956). *Taxonomy of educational objectives: The classification of educational goals: Handbook I, cognitive domain.* New York: Longmans, Green.

Butler, K. (1986). *Learning and teaching style: In theory and in practice.* (2nd ed.). Columbia, CT: Learners Dimension.

Dick, W., Carey, L., & Carey, J. (2001). *The systematic design of instruction.* (5th ed.). New York: Addison-Wesley Educational Publishers.

Dunn, R., & Dunn, K. (1992). *Teaching elementary students through their individual learning styles: Practical applications for grades 3–6.* Boston: Allyn and Bacon.

Gagné, R. (1985). *The conditions of learning and theory of instruction.* (4th ed.). New York: Holt, Rinehart and Winston.

Koontz, F. R. (1996). *Media and technology in the classroom.* (5th ed.). Dubuque, IA: Kendall/Hunt.

Morrison, G., Ross, S., & Kemp, J. (2004). *Designing effective instruction.* (4th ed.). Hoboken, NJ: John Wiley & Sons.

Smaldino, S., Russell, J., Heinich, R., & Molenda, M. (2005). *Instructional technology and media for learning.* (8th ed.). Upper Saddle River, NJ: Pearson/Merrill/Prentice Hall.

Smith, P. L., & Ragan, T. J. (1999). *Instructional design.* (2nd ed.). Upper Saddle River, NJ: Merrill.

CHAPTER 5

Step 2: State Performance Objectives for E-learning

CHAPTER OUTLINE

The Sinking of the *Bismarck*
The Need for Performance Objectives
The Elements of a Performance Objective
    Student
    Skills
    Supplies
    Standards
Rules for Writing Performance Objectives
Hierarchical Learning
Performance Objective Exercise
Summary
Key to Performance Objective Exercise
Case Studies
    Course Description No. 1
      Performance Objectives
    Course Description No. 2
      Performance Objectives
    Course Description No. 3
      Performance Objectives
References

KNOWLEDGE OBJECTIVES

At the end of this chapter, you should be able to:

1. Support, with examples, the five reasons for need of performance objectives for each e-lesson with 100% accuracy.
2. Define performance objective according to established criteria.
3. Identify the four elements of a performance objective with 100% accuracy.
4. Describe the importance of the two criteria for establishing standards according the established criteria.
5. Defend the notion that performance objectives may be changed as the Web-based instruction is being designed with 100% accuracy.
6. Explain why vague behaviors, such as to appreciate, to understand, to enjoy, to know, and the like, should not be used in performance objectives according to established criteria.
7. Evaluate the rules for writing performance objectives by writing examples of incorrectly written objectives for each rule with 100% accuracy.
8. Explain why some students do not prefer "cold storage" of information.
9. Define hierarchical learning with 100% accuracy.
10. Explain why, when designing performance objectives, it is the goal to write the objective at the highest possible level according to the given information.

(continued)

(*continued*)

LEXICON

Terms to know:

analysis	qualitative criteria
application	quantitative criteria
comprehension	skill
evaluation	standards
hierarchical learning	student
knowledge	supplies
learned outcomes	synthesis
performance objective	

THE SINKING OF THE *BISMARCK*

During World War II, on May 24, 1941, at 6:00 a.m., the *Bismarck*, the largest German battleship ever built, fired its huge 15-inch guns at the HMS *Hood* of the British Royal Navy (Lotthouse, 2001). At a range of 25,000 yards, one salvo had a direct hit on the *Hood*, sinking her in just three minutes.

The Royal Navy, in a concentrated effort to locate and sink the *Bismarck*, ordered the aircraft carrier HMS *Arc Royal* and the HMS *Sheffield*, which were at Gibraltar, to immediately sail and engage the *Bismarck* and sink her as quickly as possible.

On May 26 at 8:30 p.m., the second attack of Swordfish aircraft left the *Arc Royal*. Fifteen aircraft attacked the *Bismarck* but only two of the fifteen torpedoes found their mark. The first hit at amidships, causing no damage. The second hit the stern of the *Bismarck*, jamming the rudder. The ship was unable to steer a course of action.

By early morning May 27, the *Sheffield* noticed that the *Bismarck* was traveling in a wide circle and was not able to control its course. The Royal Navy took advantage of this and in two hours two Royal Navy battleships reduced the *Bismarck* to a blazing hulk. At 10:40 a.m., the *Bismarck* slipped beneath the waves.

THE NEED FOR PERFORMANCE OBJECTIVES

The *Bismarck* had no control of its direction after the torpedo struck its rudder. To prevent an online lesson from being developed with no control of direction, you need to write performance objectives to guide the students.

Just as a builder needs a detailed blueprint to construct a building, you will need well-defined objectives to design your instruction.

You will recall that in the last chapter we discussed the development of goals that are very general and broad statements of what the student should be able to do at the end of the entire course. A performance objective, however, is a clear, precise, and well-defined statement that informs the students what they will be able to do as the result of the specific instruction contained in the individual lesson. Performance objectives may be referred to as a subset of course goals for each lesson. You may also consider the development of individual performance objectives for the lessons as tentative and can be changed as necessary as the instruction is developed. The objective may be revised at any time during the design process as necessary.

There are five important reasons for designing performance objectives:

1. To concentrate on learning outcomes of the students
2. To make the proper selection of lesson content
3. To determine the best design and delivery strategy
4. To select the appropriate mediated instruction that will reinforce the performance objectives
5. To create a framework for devising ways to evaluate the students

To assist in the proper development of performance objectives for your online session, it will help to first think of the output of the lesson or the skills the students will need to learn, that is, the learning outcome of the lesson. If you concentrate on what the students will learn, it will become a much easier task for you to select the appropriate lesson content (see chapter 8) that will enable the student to obtain the required skill. Lesson content may be found in the selected text for the course and in the literature, as well as in an Internet search for updated content material. Once the appropriate behavior (more on this in an upcoming section) has been chosen and appropriate lesson content has been selected and developed, you can now determine the best design and teaching strategy to present the material in your online lesson (see chapter 8). Again, care should be taken in the methodology by which the content is presented to the learners, keeping in mind the various learning styles of the students. The use of varied teaching strategies will also assist your students who have varied learning styles. Next, as the lesson content is developed, consideration should be given to the types of mediated instruction (see chapter 8) that may be incorporated into the online lesson that will reinforce the performance objective. This mediated instruction will provide cuing devices to learn and recall the skill to be learned. Finally, the performance objective will enable you to evaluate the student (see chapter 11) as to how much they have been able to learn and the degree of mastery.

THE ELEMENTS OF A PERFORMANCE OBJECTIVE

A properly written performance objective consists of four basic components: the student, the skills to be learned, the supplies that will be needed to obtain the skill, and the standards by which students will be evaluated. This is referred to as the *4 S method of analysis*.

Student

The student must first be identified to ensure the performance objective will be written for the proper level as well as for the specific course. The identification of the student in the performance objective is the easiest to perform; for example, *the engineering student, the early childhood student, the biology student*, and so on identifies the student for whom the performance objective is written. As you progress in writing your objectives it is very acceptable to identify the student simply as "you."

Skills

Performance objectives must include the new skill or performance behavior. These are verbs that describe the skill to be learned such as analyze, contrast, evaluate, and so on. Basically, two rules must be observed in the selection process of the behavior. The first rule is that the skill must be *observable*, that is, you must be able to observe the performance of the skill. If the performance cannot be observed, a different and more appropriate behavior must be selected. The second rule is that the skill must be *measurable*. Some type of criteria must be established to accurately measure the skill. If you cannot determine precisely how to measure this skill in order to measure the knowledge gained toward completing the performance objective, then a different skill or behavior must be selected.

You probably have read objectives that contain behaviors as *to know, to understand, to appreciate, to enjoy*, or *to have greater faith in*. These behaviors are vague and ambiguous, and cannot be measured. For example, in an art appreciation class, the instructor writes in the syllabus: "The student will *appreciate* the artwork of the French painter Monet, who lived from 1840 to 1926 and is known for his painting *Water Lilies.*" At the end of the course, the student, who is failing, confronts the instructor and claims that he does in fact appreciate Monet's artwork and deserves an A in the class. According to the performance objective contained in the syllabus, the instructor should give the student an A in the course since the student has declared his appreciation for the artist. This objective sounds absurd, but nevertheless, it is a true argument.

Box 5.1 shows some very specific performance behaviors that can be measured.

Box 5.1   Measurable Performance Behaviors

add	defend	kick	reduce	analyze
define	label	remove	apply	describe
locate	demonstrate	build	diagram	make
select	choose	distinguish	translate	weigh
multiply	state	compare	explain	graph
illustrate	write	list	define	evaluate

Supplies

The students must be informed about what will be given to them in order to complete the objective. In a math class, it may be a calculator. In a science class, it may be a microscope. In courses dealing with theory, it may be information. Generally, the performance objective begins with what the student will be given, for example: *Given a PowerPoint program, the student will design a presentation.* In this case, the student will be given a PowerPoint program. Note carefully that some givens or supplies do not have to be written. In this case, it is obvious that the student will have a computer to use the program.

Standards

This is the level at which the student will be evaluated. Standards may also be called criteria or degree. Setting standards is slightly more difficult than identifying the class for whom the objective was written or the supplies needed.

Standards are grouped into two basic forms: qualitative and quantitative criteria. Qualitative criteria deal with how well the student has performed or the quality of performance. For the majority of qualitative performance objectives, you may write them with *100% accuracy*. This may be the standard. When 100% is used, it means that anything less than scoring 100 on that performance objective will mean a reduction in points. Depending upon the degree of difficulty, the standard may be less. For example, the criteria may be 80% or even 70%. Some performance objectives are written with 70% accuracy, meaning it is a pass-or-fail objective. Any score that is 70% or higher is acceptable. Whatever the percentage value that is set, it is your responsibility to set the level at which the students must perform.

Quantitative criteria deal with how much the student has been able to accomplish, and in some cases there may be a time limit for the performance. Again, you will establish the quantitative criteria that would be appropriate for the performance objective.

Let's look at this example of criteria: *Given six media, the student will correctly demonstrate three media within 9 minutes with 70% accuracy.*

In this example, both qualitative and quantitative criteria are used. For the qualitative criterion, the student must perform at the 70% level. For the quantitative criterion, the student must demonstrate three media within 9 minutes. The 9-minute criterion is used for a reason. This will keep the student from trying to demonstrate the media using a trial-and-error method. On average, it would take about 3 minutes for a student to set up and demonstrate a particular electronic medium, for example, an overhead projector or slide projector. Therefore, it is necessary to include the 9-minute criterion.

Here is another example; identify the criterion: *Given a computer, the student will demonstrate the proper procedure for booting the computer.*

This is a subtle criterion of one word: *the*. There is only one way to boot a computer. Therefore, the student demonstrating *the* proper way for booting the computer becomes the criterion. In addition, other subtle one-word criteria can be used, for example, *each*, *every*, or *all*.

You will notice that the term *correctly* is used in the first example and the term *proper* is used in the second performance objective example. You need to use these terms to eliminate confusion. For example, if you were to write: *The student will place the 35mm slide in the slide tray*, the student may place the slide in the tray, but not in the correct manner. There are eight ways to insert a slide in a slide tray, but only one correct way. Therefore, a better way to phrase this objective would be to insert the term *correctly* before the word *place*. It would then read like this: *The student will correctly place the 35mm slide in the slide tray.*

RULES FOR WRITING PERFORMANCE OBJECTIVES

When writing performance objectives, you must avoid numerous pitfalls. Many of these are subtle and often go unnoticed. Here are eight rules that will help you to write correct performance objectives.

> *Rule 1: Performance objectives must be written for learned outcomes and not evaluate a student's opinions or judgment.* If you ask for the opinion or judgment of the students, anything they say, perform, or write would be considered correct. The purpose of the performance objective is to evaluate what the students have learned or the output of the objective and not their opinion or judgment of the material or subject.
>
> *Rule 2: The objective must be student centered and at no time should the title of teacher, instructor, professor, and the like, be included in the objective.* It must be remembered that performance objectives are written for student performance. The teacher's performance is not being evaluated. You need to concentrate on what the student will be performing or learning and being evaluated on and not what you will be doing.
>
> *Rule 3: The selected behavior must be appropriate for the required skill to be learned.* Once the behavior has been selected, it will become necessary to determine the appropriateness of the behavior. The selected skill to be learned must match the performance. For example, the objective 'the student will *demonstrate appropriate design principles for a PowerPoint slide*' is acceptable. You will observe that *demonstrate* is the behavior and *appropriate design principles for a PowerPoint slide* is the skill to be learned. There is agreement between the selected skill and what the student will be demonstrating.
>
> *Rule 4: Terms such as* to believe, to have greater faith, to know, to understand, *and* to appreciate *describe behaviors that cannot be measured.* No procedures exist to measure these vague and misleading terms. Selected behaviors must be observable as well as measurable. If the selected behavior does not meet these two criteria, a different behavior must be selected.
>
> *Rule 5: Performance objectives must be obtainable and realistic.* There must be a match between how much the student can accomplish in learning the skill and the requirements of the performance objective. The level of performance should be placed slightly above the per-

formance level of the students to create a learning challenge. If, however, the requirement is too high or even too low, students may evaluate the level as either unobtainable or not challenging and may not attempt to learn the new skill. The performance objectives should also be realistic and relevant. Students soon become annoyed with learning a skill that cannot be applied, especially graduate-level students. In graduate-level courses, cold storage skills, that is, skills that are learned and are stored for later use, sometimes are not desirable (Smaldino et al., 2005). The graduate student may not understand the value in learning something that will be stored, having no guarantee that it will ever be used. However, just-in-time learning, the more pragmatic type of performance objective, is welcomed since the student can apply the skill almost immediately.

Rule 6: Performance objectives are not written for examinations. Test questions come from performance objectives and are administered after the performance has been introduced. You may want to write your test questions for a midterm or final exam as you complete the writing of your performance objectives. Therefore, writing a performance objective for a test is inappropriate.

Rule 7: Students must be evaluated in the same manner in which they are instructed. Cognitive information given to students may be evaluated in the traditional way of testing by using a written examination. If, however, a skill was demonstrated to students, they must demonstrate the skill for the evaluation. For example, if students were asked to take a true-or-false or a multiple-choice test to examine their ability to use a microscope, this would not accurately measure students' abilities. These examinations would test students' cognitive ability and not their motor skill ability of the actual operation of the microscope. In addition, to take a written test for this examination, students also could guess the correct answers to the test questions. As a result, students still may not be able to correctly operate the microscope.

Rule 8: Performance objectives are not written as an activity. There is a distinct difference between a performance skill to be learned and an activity that is used to learn the skill. It must be remembered that the purpose of the performance objective is to have the students learn a specific skill. An activity is a way to practice the skill to be learned. For example, if you were to write, "The student, given a microscope, will demonstrate the proper procedure for focusing on a slide using various powers with 100% accuracy," this would be a properly written objective. If you were to write, "The student, given a microscope, will identify three types of viruses with 100% accuracy," it becomes an activity or even a test item. In order to identify the viruses, the student would have had to develop the skill to focus the microscope.

HIERARCHICAL LEARNING

When designing instruction for an e-learning session, it is a rare event that time is taken to design specific learning outcomes. Certainly, performance objectives are designed, but little or no thought is given to the level of learning that will be taught and learned. The majority of objectives are written at the lowest levels of learning, that is, the knowledge level or the comprehension level. Little time or no time is spent at the application level, for instance, giving a student a problem that must be solved applying previously learned rules. Even less time is spent at the levels of analysis, synthesis, and evaluation. If the instructor is designing a session that incorporates mathematical concepts, the application level should be used. However, when this type of content is not being designed, little application is designed into the lesson plan. The students spend most of their time memorizing facts, terms, meaning of terms, and so on, then reproducing them for a test.

You will recall the definition for learning: *Learning is the process whereby a person has a lasting change in behavior as a result of an experience* (Gage & Berliner, 1988). Learning takes time and the change must be lasting or learning has not taken place. Learning has taken place when the behavior has changed, that is, the students have learned a new skill.

In his *Taxonomy of Educational Objectives*, Bloom (1956) created and classified levels of learning. It has been widely used in colleges of education to explain the levels of learning and the levels with which you can design your instruction.

The following is a bottom-up classification, that is, from the knowledge level, the lowest level of learning, to evaluation, which is the highest level of learning.

6. *Evaluation—using criteria to evaluate performance; testing*

Example behaviors: judge, appraise, evaluate, rate, revise, score, assess, estimate, choose, measure, select, value

Example of an evaluation objective: The student, given a course textbook, will evaluate and, if necessary, revise the written objectives of each chapter according to established criteria (Koontz, 1996).

5. *Synthesis—putting parts together and looking at the whole; writing, composing, designing a proposal*

   Example behaviors: compose, plan, propose, design, formulate, arrange, assemble, collect, construct, create, set up, organize, manage, prepare

   Example of a synthesis objective: The student, given a textbook, will design appropriate objectives for each chapter with 100% accuracy.

4. *Analysis—breaking into components; comparing and contrasting*

   Example behaviors: distinguish, analyze, calculate, experiment, test, compare, contrast, criticize, diagram, inspect, debate, inventory, question, relate, solve, examine, categorize

   Example of an analysis objective: Given example objectives, the student will categorize the parts of the objective according to the student, skill, supplies, and standards with 100% accuracy.

3. *Application—given a new situation, solving a problem*

   Example behaviors: interpret, apply, employ, use, demonstrate, dramatize, practice, illustrate, operate, schedule, shop, sketch

   Example of an application objective: The student will demonstrate how to write a properly constructed performance objective with 100% accuracy.

2. *Comprehension—organizing, translating, explaining*

   Example behaviors: translate, restate, discuss, describe, recognize, explain, express, identify, locate, report, review, state main ideas

   Example of a comprehension objective: Given information on the construction of a performance objective, the student will identify the parts of an objective with 100% accuracy

1. *Knowledge—memorizing; recalling facts, names, steps*

   Examples behaviors: define, repeat, record, list, recall, name, relate, underline, match, label, select

   Example knowledge objective: Given information on writing objectives, the student will define performance objective according to established criteria.

PERFORMANCE OBJECTIVE EXERCISE

Evaluate the following performance objectives. Make the necessary corrections using the 4 S method: student, skill, supplies, and standards. Refer to the appropriate rule for writing the performance objective. Then evaluate the level of learning according to Bloom's *Taxonomy*. The key to this exercise may be found at the end of the chapter.

1. The student will present the four most interesting causes of teaching problems.
2. Listen, with eyes open, while the teacher lists four parts of a performance objective.
3. Given a presentation on the systematic development of e-instruction, the student will appreciate the use of performance objectives when designing a session for e-learning.
4. Given a list of 10 performance objectives, the student will correctly identify the 5 that are written according to the 4 S method.
5. The student will circle all of the given behaviors.
6. The student will define the term *performance objective* using no aids.
7. The student, given 20 true-or-false statements concerning the correct operating procedure of a microscope as listed in the textbook, will correctly label 16 of these statements.
8. The student will describe, in writing, the correct procedure for operating a microscope according to established criteria.
9. Given a microscope in operable condition, the teacher will display 10 unusual and interesting slides for the student in order for the student to understand the concepts of identifying a virus.
10. Given a list of 10 possible performance objectives, the student will correctly identify all missing components, if any, in 8 of the statements, according to the criteria established in the 4 S method.

SUMMARY

There are five important reasons for designing performance objectives: (1) to concentrate on learning outcomes of the students, (2) to make the proper selection of lesson content, (3) to determine the best design and delivery strategy, (4) to select the appropriate mediated instruction that will reinforce the performance objectives, and (5) to create a framework for devising ways to evaluate the students.

Correctly written performance objectives consist of four basic parts: the student, the skills to be learned, the supplies that will be needed to obtain the skill, and the standards by which the student will be evaluated. This is referred to as the 4 S method of analysis. The student is the learner who is in the class. The skill is the behavior the student will be able to do as a result of the lesson. The supplies are what is given to the student to complete the objective, and the standard refers to how the student will be evaluated.

Specific rules have been designed for writing performance objectives. These include:

Rule 1: Performance objectives must be written for learned outcomes and not evaluate a student's opinions or judgment.

Rule 2: The objective must be student centered and at no time should the title of teacher, instructor, professor, and the like, be included in the objective.

Rule 3: The selected behavior must be appropriate for the required skill to be learned.

Rule 4: Terms such as *to believe*, *to have greater faith*, *to know*, *to understand*, and *to appreciate* describe behaviors that cannot be measured.

Rule 5: Performance objectives must be obtainable and realistic

Rule 6: Performance objectives are not written for examinations.

Rule 7: Students must be evaluated in the same manner in which they are instructed.

Rule 8: Performance objectives are not written as an activity.

An instructor must consider the level of learning when writing a performance objective. Hierarchical learning is the classification of the types of learning. These levels include, from the highest to the lowest: evaluation, synthesis, analysis, application, comprehension, and knowledge. The goal is to write objectives at as high of a level as possible when designing instruction so that it will not only challenge students but will also enable students to use the new skill in a variety of conditions.

KEY TO PERFORMANCE OBJECTIVE EXERCISE

1. *The student will present the four most interesting causes of teaching problems.*

1.1 Using the 4 S method of analysis, all parts of the objective are present. Remember, supplies or givens do not always have to be stated. In this case, it is assumed that the students were given the information. Now we need to analyze the appropriateness of each of the parts.

1.2 The skill to be learned, *present the four most interesting causes of teaching problems* has two basic problems. First, the verb *present* creates a problem. In a large class, a class management problem would arise if all students were to orally present their answers. There may not be sufficient class time. Next, if students were to orally present the four most interesting causes of teaching problems, there would be a "copycat" problem. After the first student gave his answer and was correct, all other students would do the same. In addition, the phrase *the four most interesting causes of teaching problems* is subjective, especially the words *most interesting*. What is interesting to one student may not be interesting to other students.

1.3 The standard selected is *the*, assuming there are only four causes of teaching problems. There are many more. A qualitative standard needs to be included, such as *with 100% accuracy.*

1.4 To rewrite this performance objective, it could be written as: *The student, given a list of teaching problems, will identify four problems with 100% accuracy.*

1.5 This objective violates Rule 1.

1.6 The level of learning is the knowledge level.

2. *Listen, with eyes open, while the teacher lists the four parts of a performance objective.*

   2.1 Analysis of the 4 S method indicates there is no student identified and the objective has a partial standard.

   2.2 The supplies or condition is misleading: *Listen, with eyes open.* This does not state what the student will be supplied. Next, *teacher* is used rather than *student*. Although the standard used is *the*, it should also have a qualitative standard.

   2.3 To rewrite this performance objective, it could be written as: *The student will list the four parts of an objective with 100% accuracy.*

2.4 This objective violates Rule 2.

2.5 The level of learning is the knowledge level.

3. *Given a presentation on the systematic development of e-instruction, the student will appreciate the use of performance objectives when designing a session for e-learning.*

   3.1 Using the 4 S method of analysis, an inappropriate skill is used and no standards are indicated. The term *appreciate* is not a skill that can be measured.

   3.2 To rewrite this performance objective, it could be written as: *Given a presentation on systematic development of e-instruction, the student will design appropriate performance objectives for a session for e-learning according to established criteria.*

   3.3 This objective violates Rule 4.

   3.4 The level of learning is the synthesis level.

4. *Given a list of 10 performance objectives, the student will correctly identify the 5 that are written according to the 4 S method.*

   4.1 Using the 4 S method of analysis, all four parts of the objective are appropriately written.

   4.2 This performance objective appears to be an activity rather than a performance objective since the student would have had to learn the four parts of a performance objective. This is more of a drill-and-practice exercise in the process of identification.

   4.3 To rewrite this performance objective, it could be written as: *The student will correctly identify all parts of a performance objective using the 4 S method according to established criteria.*

   4 4 This objective violates Rule 8.

   4.5 The level of learning is the knowledge level.

5. *The student will circle all of the given behaviors.*

   5.1 Using the 4 S method of analysis, all parts of the performance objective are present.

   5.2 The skill selected is inappropriate. The output of this objective is obtaining the skill of circling behaviors. It should be identifying behaviors. The standard is subtle, using the term *all*.

   5.3 To rewrite this performance objective, it could be written as: *Given a list, the student will identify skills that are appropriate to use in performance objectives with 100% accuracy.*

5.4 This objective does not violate any rules.

5.5 The level of learning is the knowledge level.

6. *The student will define the term* performance objective *using no aids.*

    6.1 Using the 4 S method of analysis, this performance objective lacks only standards. It is assumed that the supplies or givens is the definition of *performance objective.* However, the phrase *using no aids* may make this appear to be a test question.

    6.2 To rewrite this performance objective, it could be written as: *The student will describe all of the parts of a performance objective according to established criteria.*

    6.3 This objective violates Rule 6.

    6.3 The level of learning is the comprehension level.

7. *The student, given 20 true-or-false statements concerning the correct operating procedure of a microscope as listed in the textbook, will correctly label 16 of these statements.*

    7.1 Using the 4 S method of analysis, the only missing part is the standard. However, there are several inappropriate parts. First, the skill selected, label true or false, is incorrect. A student cannot label a true-or-false statement. The student would identify each statement as true or false. Second, this performance objective is written as a test. Third, it is inappropriate to take a written test when the skill was demonstrated.

    7.2 To rewrite this performance objective, it could be written as: *The student will demonstrate the correct operating procedure of a microscope with 100% accuracy.*

    7.3 This objective violates Rules 3, 6, and 7.

    7.4 The level of learning is the application level.

8. *The student will describe, in writing, the correct procedure for operating a microscope according to established criteria.*

    8.1 Using the 4 S method of analysis, all parts of the performance objective are included. However, it would be inappropriate for the student to describe the procedure for operating the microscope. It is appropriate to have the student to demonstrate the procedure.

    8.2 To rewrite this performance objective, it could be written as: *The student will demonstrate the correct procedure of operating a microscope according to established criteria.*

8.3 This objective violates Rule 7.

8.4 The level of learning is the application level.

9. *Given a microscope in operable condition, the teacher will display 10 unusual and interesting slides for the student in order for the student to understand the concepts of identifying a virus.*

   9.1 Using the 4 S method of analysis, no student is identified, the skill selected is incorrect, supplies were inappropriate, and there is no standard.

   9.2 Obviously, *teacher* must be changed to *student*. The supplies also is incorrect. There is no reason to state that the microscope is in operable condition unless the student is being required to identify a mechanical problem with the microscope. There is a need to change the skill and eliminate the subjective phrase *display 10 unusual and interesting slides* as well as *the student to understand the concepts of identifying a virus. To understand* cannot be measured. It is not clear from this performance objective as to what skill is required. Also, this appears to be an activity and not a skill to be learned since the student is required to display 10 slides.

   9.3 To rewrite this performance objective, it could be written as: *The student, given a microscope, will describe a virus contained on a slide with 100% accuracy.*

   9.4 This objective violates Rules 2, 3, and 4.

   9.5 The level of learning is at the comprehension level.

10. *Given a list of 10 possible performance objectives, the student will correctly identify all missing components, if any, in 8 of the statements, according to the criteria established in the 4 S method.*

    10.1 Using the 4 S method of analysis, this performance objective contains all the required parts of an objective.

    10.2 This performance objective is either written for a test or is an activity.

    10.3 To rewrite this performance objective, it could be written as: *Given a performance objective, the student will evaluate the correctness of each of the parts of the objective using the 4 S method of analysis with 100% accuracy.*

    10.4 This objective violates Rules 6 and 8.

    10.5 The level of learning is the evaluation level.

CASE STUDIES

Course Description No. 1

Course: BIOL 6000/8000 Introduction to Scientific Thought and Expression
Instructor: Dr. Earnest DuBrul, associate professor, biology

Performance Objectives

Students will be able to:

1. Contrast an explanation and a hypothesis supported by controlled experiments.
2. Evaluate the claim that most theories are impermanent.
3. Demonstrate that the precision of all physical measurement is limited.
4. Explain that mathematics allows one to abstract generalities and deal with general relations.
5. Demonstrate knowledge of basic statistics and probability and how they apply to the provisional nature of science.
6. Demonstrate knowledge of an experimental and historical approach to supporting hypotheses.
7. Examine a number of important discoveries in various scientific disciplines in the original literature in order to determine the limits and ramification of science.

Course Description No. 2

Course: MET 3100 Applied Thermodynamics
Instructor: Dr. Ella Fridman, associate professor, engineering technology

Performance Objectives

Performance objectives are written as questions.

General:

1. Why do most cars have gasoline engines?
2. What are the advantages and disadvantages of two-stroke engines?
3. How does the cycle diagram for two-stroke engines differ from the cycle diagram for four-stroke engines?

(continued)

(*continued*)

Specific performance questions:

1. How does the diesel engine differ from the gasoline engine?
2. How does the temperature ratio T1/T2 relate to the compression ratio V1/V2?
3. How does the temperature ratio T3/T1 relate to the cutoff ratio of rc=v3/V2?

Course Description No. 3

Course: CIEC 3200 Philosophy and Practice in Early Childhood Education
Instructor: Dr. Bob Cryan, professor, early childhood education

Performance Objectives

Given the information contained in the textbook and lecture notes, the student will, with 100% accuracy:

1. Describe the learning processes in early childhood education.
2. Examine the features of authentic learning.
3. Explore learner-centered teaching and learning and explain the cycle of learning.
4. Describe the major learning theories and their implications for the very young.
5. Examine the influence of teachers' beliefs on their teaching practice.
6. Describe the central role of play in children's learning.

REFERENCES

Bloom, B. (Ed.). (1956). *Taxonomy of educational objectives: The classification of educational goals: Handbook I, cognitive domain.* New York: Longmans, Green.

Gage, N., & Berliner, D. (1988). *Educational psychology.* (4th ed.). Boston: Houghton Mifflin.

Koontz, F. R. (1996). *Media and technology in the classroom.* (5th ed.). Dubuque, IA: Kendall/Hunt.

Lofthouse, A. (2001). *Sink the Bismark . . . not the Sheffield.* Sheffnet. http://www.sheffnet.co.uk/default.asp?contentid=424

Smaldino, S., Russell, J., Heinich, R., & Molenda, M. (2005). *Instructional technology and media for learning.* (8th ed.). Upper Saddle River, NJ: Pearson/Merrill/Prentice Hall.

CHAPTER 6

Step 3: Select Instructional Materials, Organize Content, and Media

---

CHAPTER OUTLINE

Selecting Instructional Content
  Enabling Objectives
  Search Methods for Content
Order Instructional Content
Select Appropriate Support Material
Design a Summary
Introduction
Summary of Order of Preparation for Lesson Content
How Students Learn
Learning Benefits From Instructional Media
  Instructional Media Creates a Direct Substitute for the Real Learning Experience
  Instructional Media Creates Accurate Communication
  Instructional Media Creates Alternatives for Learning
  Instructional Media Creates Excitement and Curiosity in Learning
Selection Criteria for Instructional Media
Selecting Specific Instructional Media for TPO Reinforcement
Whiteboard Technology
  The Document Camera
  PowerPoint and Macromedia Flash
  Additional Media
Summary
Case Studies
  Course Description No. 1
    The 5 Es Approach
  Course Description No. 2
  Course Description No. 3
References

KNOWLEDGE OBJECTIVES

At the end of this chapter, you should be able to:

1. Compare and contrast enabling objectives and terminal performance objectives according to established criteria.
2. Construct a search process for appropriate content for a distance-learning online lesson.
3. Explain how Boolean logic assists in locating pertinent lesson content according to the text.
4. Identify the three orders of organizing online lesson content.
5. Describe the importance of using appropriate support material.

(continued)

(*continued*)

6. Describe the purpose of using a summary for an online lesson.
7. Identify the purposes of an introduction for an online lesson.
8. Describe how students learn using examples from Dale's Cone of Experience.
9. Contrast the primary and secondary ways of learning new cognate material according to Dale.
10. Summarize the learning benefits from using instructional media.
11. Justify the selection criteria for the selection of instructional media.
12. Identify and describe three instructional media that can be used for an online course.

LEXICON

Terms to know:

abstract	iconic
advance organizer	instructional media
auditory learning	photo CD
Boolean operators	PowerPoint
CD-ROM	search engine
chronological order	sequential order
document camera	terminal performance objective
DVD-ROM	topical order
enabling objective	visual learning
enactive	whiteboard technology

You have now covered the first two important steps in the ASSIST-Me model. The first step was to analyze the course selection, curriculum, instructional setting, and student. The second step was to develop performance objectives. In this section, you will select the content for the individual online lesson, appropriately organize the content, and select media that will reinforce the performance objective.

SELECTING INSTRUCTIONAL CONTENT

Enabling Objectives

Select one of your performance objectives for an individual session and divide it into subparts or enabling objectives (Gagné, 1985). All performance objectives can and should be divided into smaller objectives, or steps, which will allow the student to learn the cognate material in smaller chunks. As these enabling objectives are learned, the students will be able to learn the end result or the output of the objective. This is referred to as the terminal performance objective, or TPO. Therefore, you have, for each distance-learning session, one or more TPOs, and each TPO will have its

own enabling objectives. You may think of enabling objectives as building blocks. When all of the building blocks are completed, you have some
type of a completed structure, in this case, a performance objective that
has been learned by the student. For example, *The student will correctly
identify all parts of a performance objective using the 4 S method according to established criteria.* In this case, students must learn to identify
the individual parts of an objective, that is, the student, the skill, the supplies, and the standards. Each of these parts is an enabling objective to
learn the terminal performance objective.

Search Methods for Content

The process of selecting appropriate instructional content material that
will reinforce the performance objectives becomes extremely important.
A plethora of information is at your disposal. Content material can obviously be obtained from the textbook you are using for the course as well
as other textbooks and notes from other courses you have taken. A good
source for additional material is the references at the end of the chapter.
However, one resource that should not be overlooked to locate new, stimulating, and even controversial material, is the Internet.

When you begin a search on the Internet for lesson content, you will use
a search engine (Harris, 2000) that provides keyword search capability of
registered Web sites. Common search engines include Google, AltaVista,
Yahoo, and WebCrawler. You should use more than one search engine because different engines will locate different information and sources. No
one search engine looks for all of the material. Therefore, it is wise not to
base an entire distance education session on a single resource.

Here are some major search engines that will assist you in locating your
lesson content.

- *AltaVista* (www.altavista.com) is a search engine that has a large
  database based on the full text of Web pages. This site is recommended for specific terms, obscure places of information, long or unusual phrases, complex keyword searches, and extensive or serious
  research projects.
- *Hotbot* (www.hotbot.com) is the second of the two largest database
  search engines. This site is recommended for beginners as well as experienced searchers who want an extensive database for very specific
  terms and obscure pieces of information. Searches may also be re-

stricted to a region or timeframe of material, for example, last week, last month, and so on.

- *Northern Light* (www.northernlight.com) has a database of periodical articles for a fee. It has over 45,000 journal reviews, books, magazines, and newswires not readily found on the Web (Smaldino et al., 2005). This site is recommended for exact phrase searches, scholarly topics, and topics likely to be found in professional journals.
- *Excite* (www.excite.com) has a medium-sized database and includes current news articles from more than 300 periodicals. Excite is recommended for current events and topics involving politics, society, culture, and assessing general subjects content.
- *Infoseek* (www.infoseek.go.com) is recommended for current events and uses keyword searching.
- *Lycos* (www.lycos.com) has a combination search engine and directory. Lycos is recommended for locating sites that have been rated highly by reviews and locating pictures and images.
- *Google* (www.google.com) has a very large database and is a very popular site for locating academic material as well as pictures and graphics.
- *Yahoo* (www.yahoo.com) is the oldest and best-known directory. This site is small compared with the other search engines, but content is very good and well organized. Yahoo is recommended for searching for sites by subject or academic area and finding lists of resources.
- *Galaxy* (www.galaxy.tradewave.com) is designed for searches of scholarly subject matter. Main entries include engineering, law, medicine, and social science. This site is suitable for the serious searcher.

It must be remembered that Web sites change daily, as does the database of information that is searched. If the relevant information is not found in the first 20 hits, try another search. It may also be helpful to use a metasearch engine such as Metacrawler (www.metacrawler.com), Search.com (www.search.com), Dogpile (www.dogpile.com), or Beaucoup (www.beaucoup.com) to search for your session content.

To further increase your information retrieval (Harris, 2000), it may be necessary to use some specific search phrases found in Boolean operators (Boolean logic). When it is appropriate, you may want to use some or all of these terms:

- AND: both terms must be in the document; as a restrictor, e.g., distance education

- OR: a hit will be made of one or both terms; may exclude pages you want to see
- NOT (sometimes AND NOT): a restrictor; use NOT carefully for it may exclude valuable hits
- NEAR (AltaVista supports this): locates terms within 10 words of each other
- Nesting: descriptor AND (descriptor OR descriptor); e.g., childbirth AND (natural OR at home)
- Quotation marks: ". . ."; limits search to an exact word search
- Wildcards: return searches with near hits using an asterisk; e.g., "Renaissance prints*" will yield print, prints, printers, printing, etc.
- Pipes (Infoseek supports this): vertical bars separating search terms; e.g., aircraft|cost|parts|bolts|

ORDER INSTRUCTIONAL CONTENT

After you have downloaded your material and reviewed the textbook to be used for the course, similar textbooks, and notes from various allied courses for lesson content, it is now time to organize all of this material into an effective design. One of the major concerns is to limit the number of terminal performance objectives for each lesson as well as material for each of the enabling objectives and to place this material in some type of order. Content may be placed into three major categories: chronological, sequential, or topical order.

Chronological order refers to a sequence in time, such as dates as in years, months, days, or specific times of the day. For material that may be in a step-by-step order, sequential order will be used. Sequential steps are found in solving statistical problems, math problems, chemistry equations, and the like. Topical order, however, is found most frequently. Here, the material does not have any special order. You, as a designer, are free to order the content in the most interesting manner.

SELECT APPROPRIATE SUPPORT MATERIAL

Once the order has been selected, it is time to generate an outline of the material to be included in the lesson. In this outline, you will obviously include the downloaded content material as well as text material to be learned. Pure content material, many times, is difficult to understand, retain, and apply, and is often boring. To help in the learning process, you will need to locate and design support material for this information that will serve as cuing devices to remember lesson content. These cuing devices may be *illustrations*, *examples*, or even *hypothetical situations*. Often, to clarify a concept, the designer realizes that the learners will need an example to better understand the lesson content. Next, consider using *quotations* from other sources that will bring authenticity and clarification to the concept. It may be appropriate to use some *figures* or statistics that will better clarify the concept. Examples of these figures include concepts of time, amount, and size. *Comparisons* that illustrate similarities and *contrasts* that illustrate differences also aid in clarifying concepts. Finally, used judicially, the interjection of humor may help as a cuing device as well as creating a pleasant learning experience.

DESIGN A SUMMARY

Thus far in our design approach of lesson content, we have selected the TPO, divided it into enabling objectives, and obtained content material and support material from various sources. Our next step is to prepare a summary for our session. Often, the summary of a lesson is neglected and not considered an integral part of the lesson. However, the summary can serve as a major review for the learner. It should summarize the terminal performance objectives of the lesson. These major points briefly include the enabling objectives for each of the terminal performance objectives. You may also view the summary as the miniature chapter. It should also serve as a review of points that may not have been understood or even overlooked.

INTRODUCTION

The next task is to design an introduction to the session. This introduction serves as an attention-getting device. Just because the student has registered for the course and appears to be interested in the content, it is not a measure of the attention the student is contributing to the session. Using examples, posing questions, and showing the relevance of the content can gain student attention. The introduction can also serve as an advance organizer, in other words, informing the student of the order and content that will be presented. This advance organizer not only aids the student to look for the specific content and the order in which it will be presented, it also helps you to keep yourself organized when designing the lesson content.

SUMMARY OF ORDER OF PREPARATION
FOR LESSON CONTENT

To summarize, when designing the content of the lesson, follow these steps:

1. Select your TPOs and divide them into enabling objectives.
2. Order the TPOs.
3. Obtain and design appropriate support material for each enabling objective.
4. Complete an outline of the online lesson.
5. Prepare a summary.
6. Prepare an attention-getting introduction that contains the goal of the lesson and an advance organizer.

HOW STUDENTS LEARN

Learning psychologists such as Bruner, Gagné, Briggs, Wager, Skinner, Piaget, and others, have spent much of their lives studying the way we learn (Koontz, 1996). After years of research studies, we can state with confidence that all learners, young and old, learn in a similar manner. The difference between younger and older learners is that older learners have developed more sophisticated ways to learn.

When we begin to learn something new, the best way is to experience the learning situation by actually becoming involved. In other words, when learning a math concept, the best way to begin learning is to carefully observe a demonstration by the teacher. The students copy the problem into their notebooks and work with the teacher to solve the problem. This type of learning, also called the constructivist perspective (Simonson et al., 2003), engages students in a practical experience, that is, actual hands-on learning (see Dale's Cone of Experience). This becomes an *enactive* form of learning. Other examples of enactive learning are demonstrations, field trips, dramatizations, and contrived experiences created by the teacher. Other than the demonstration, forms of enactive learning take a long time to create and time to complete, especially the field trip.

If the enactive form of instruction does not seem to be practical, all too often, some teachers will design a lesson at the other extreme, that is, just read the material in the text and then discuss it in class. This type of learning is the most *symbolic* or abstract form of learning. The students are required to begin the learning process on their own. This, however, is a much more difficult way to learn the material because it is the opposite of what the learning psychologists tell us is the best way to learn, using the enactive or hands-on approach.

The middle ground between the enactive and abstract ways to learn is the *iconic* approach. When instruction is put into a media format, it is called the iconic form of learning. It is the bridge between the enactive and the abstract form of learning. The word *icon* in Greek means "picture." The iconic form of learning provides instruction in both visual and auditory formats. The iconic form of learning deals with learning as found in instructional television, PowerPoint presentations, graphics, and the like, for example, when viewing an instructional television lesson it creates a direct substitute for the enactive form of learning. The student can learn the new material, much like observing a demonstration or going on a field trip.

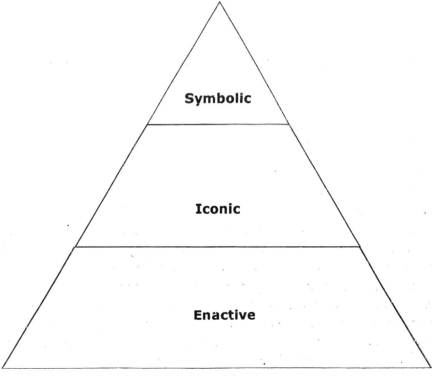

Dale's Cone of Experience

Notice that at the lower end of the learning continuum we have a very large base dealing with the enactive or hands-on learning. Here you design the direct-learning experience. At the top of the continuum is the abstract form of learning where the students are required to read the material, talk about it, and then take a test. You will notice that the iconic form of learning is placed directly in the middle of the other forms of learning and forms a bridge between the enactive and the abstract forms of learning.

LEARNING BENEFITS FROM INSTRUCTIONAL MEDIA

When you use instructional media in your online lesson (Koontz, 1996), four learning benefits will occur. Instructional media will create: (1) a direct substitute for the real learning experience, (2) accurate communication, (3) alternatives for learning, and (4) excitement and curiosity in learning.

Instructional Media Creates a Direct Substitute for the Real Learning Experience

Many times, you will not be able to create a direct or enactive learning experience for your students since the class is online. The problem of coordinating a field trip and the length of time it takes to get it organized is not practical. It also defeats the purpose of distance learning. However, a demonstration may be very practical since you could develop the demonstration and have it videotaped. It would need to be prepared only once and it could be repeatedly used.

Instructional Media Creates Accurate Communication

The news media seeks out stories and reports them back to their respective broadcast stations or newspapers. The viewers or readers have no way of knowing the accuracy of the report. If a plane crashes, one reporter may state that 200 deaths occurred. Another may state that there were more than 250. Another may report an unconfirmed number of deaths. Unless you can monitor all of these various sources, you may never know the actual death toll. Reporters get their information in slightly different ways. Some or all of the information may not be factual.

When using instructional media in your online lessons, you have more control over factual material. Let's use, for example, the Mount

Saint Helens eruption in 1980. Just prior to this eruption, several geologists were on the scene videotaping this enormous eruption. Some were on the ground while others were taping from the air. After the eruption, the videotape was reviewed and edited for a learning experience that could be used for purposes of instruction. Before the students viewed the videotaped eruption, the teacher briefed the students as to what they were going to see and gave them a series of questions they were to answer after they had seen the videotaped segment. All students were able to observe the same event. The students were able to learn some of the basics of geology and characteristics of volcanic eruptions and report the same findings.

Instructional Media Creates Alternatives for Learning

Teaching is both an art and a science. As an art, you must be extremely creative in your instructional design, not only to create instruction that is effective so that the students learn what they are supposed to learn, but instruction that is interesting and stimulates the students to learn. Teaching is also a science. Much of what we know about learning theory has been established from formal research studies. We know that each student has his or her own unique way of learning the content we have designed into our individual online lesson. Since there are multiple different learning styles, it seems logical that we would use multiple different teaching styles. The traditional "lecture" style can become extremely boring, tends to be impersonal, and leads to passive learning. If you were to take your lecture notes and write them into your online lesson, the computer would become a glorified page turner or scroller. Your approach would become very abstract. If, however, you engage your students in a variety of instructional media, which will be discussed in detail in an upcoming section, the online course is much more effective and enjoyable.

Instructional Media Creates Excitement and Curiosity in Learning

There is no substitute for the real learning experience. Learning psychologists, as it has been pointed out, state that the best way for us to learn is to be actively engaged in the material. Reading and talking about the material is not engaging or exciting. However, some teachers continue to give reading assignments and then simply discuss them in class rather than providing a direct learning experience.

For example, if a geology student who is studying the phenomena of various volcanic eruptions were to just read about various types of volcanic eruptions, it probably would not have nearly the impact as seeing and hearing a videotaped segment of the extreme power and devastation of the eruption of Mount Saint Helens. The students would observe the volcanic ash as it soars up to 30,000 feet into the atmosphere and the ash creating 12- to 18-inch drifts. The students would see, using animation, how the ash drifted across the United States and fell to the ground, causing black soot to coat everything in its path. The students would also observe the shockwave stemming from the eruption that flattened hundreds of thousands of trees as if they were mere matchsticks. Seeing an event is more interesting than just reading about the event.

SELECTION CRITERIA FOR INSTRUCTIONAL MEDIA

As the designer of your online course, you have a wide variety of instructional media from which to choose. First, you may look for instructional media that has been professionally produced. Second, if this instructional media is not available or only a segment of the produced material can be used to reinforce your objective, you can modify this material for your online instruction. You may only be able to use a segment or portion of the material. Third, if nothing is available, you can design your own material or have an instructional designer design the media for you.

Unfortunately, not all of the professionally produced instructional media can or should be used for online instruction. Instructional media selection should meet specific criteria and a systematic evaluation should be conducted for each selection.

1. *Select instructional media that reinforces terminal performance objectives.* Not all of the available produced media is designed to specifically support your performance objectives. If what you have selected does not directly reinforce your objective, do not use it. If only a segment supports your performance objective, then use just that segment. Do not use any instructional media just because it is available.

2. *Select instructional media that has accurate information.* Again, if the information found in your possible selection does not contain accurate information or the information is outdated, do not use the me-

dia. However, if the information that you would like to present is controversial and has multiple sides, you could present various instructional media and have students identify the various issues and draw a conclusion on their own.

3. *Select instructional media that engages the student.* Some instructional media may have some type of formal evaluation, that is, some designers may have conducted formative or summative evaluations on the instructional media before making it available to the public. If possible, review all evaluations carefully before adopting instructional media for your online lesson. It is not good design practice to use instructional media that is passive and does not engage the student. Passive instructional media can evoke passive learning.

4. *Select instructional media that is free from bias.* Some instructional media that is free and available for medical classes are produced by manufacturers that quietly promote their own products. Use your judgment to determine whether a piece of instructional media is an infomercial.

5. *Select instructional media that has good production quality.* No student can learn from instructional media that has poor audio or video quality. In addition, poor production quality will impede learning. A good production evaluation rule to use is that the instructional media should not call the attention of the medium used. In other words, if a student is viewing an instructional lesson and a poorly framed out-of-focus camera shot is used, the student will no longer be concentrating on the subject content but rather the poorly framed or out-of-focus camera shot. Students will compare the production quality of the instructional television lesson with a professionally produced and directed commercial program.

SELECTING SPECIFIC INSTRUCTIONAL MEDIA FOR TPO REINFORCEMENT

Through years of research, it has been discovered that the majority of students are visual learners. If you were to ask your class how many thought they were visual learners, only a few would probably think that is the primary way they learn. Their first thoughts may be of viewing something, such as an instructional television lesson, transparencies, or pictures. Most students entirely overlook the amount of time spent completing required reading in any given course. Most new material is initially learned by reading. (When reviewing Dale's Cone of Experience, you will note that the enactive part of learning constitutes the largest section.) Generally, about 85% of students are visual learners while 15% are auditory learners. The visual learners complete their learning experience by auditory reinforcement.

The use of visuals in the teaching/learning process is of great value. Visuals can translate abstract, and sometimes very vague, concepts into understandable concepts (Smaldino et al., 2005). Visuals provide a concrete reference to abstract concepts. For example, if the ASSIST-Me model were just described, it would be difficult for the reader to understand the design sequences and the interrelationships established in each of the steps. Much of the detail of the model may not be understood, recognized, or retained. However, when the ASSIST-Me model is visualized in a typical instructional design model format, the steps in the design process and the relationships that are established are more understandable and become clearer. Pictures, charts, graphs, posters, and even cartoons can reinforce abstract print media.

A variety of instructional media is available to reinforce your performance objectives. Traditional forms of media, for example, the chalkboard, overhead projector, or slide projector, are not appropriate for online instruction lessons. However, these have been replaced with smarter technology. The blackboard has been replaced with the electronic whiteboard, the overhead projector has been replaced with the document camera, and the slide projector has been replaced with PowerPoint and Macromedia Flash.

WHITEBOARD TECHNOLOGY

A whiteboard is an interactive, touch-sensitive screen that works with a computer and a video projector (http://www.smarttech.com). The computer screen is projected onto the electronic whiteboard, enabling the teacher to touch any part of the screen to perform a computer function without touching the computer keyboard or mouse. By using special computer software, the teacher is able to display produced instructional materials and can interact with these materials by highlighting or pointing to parts using an electric pen. These instructional materials can then be saved to a computer file that students can later access from the teacher's Web page. The teacher may also print copies of the class session, complete with student input, enabling students to focus on asking questions and understanding concepts rather than taking notes.

Interactive whiteboards (SMART Technologies, Inc., 2004) can be used to interact with electronic content and multimedia in a multiperson learning environment. Various learning activities can include:

- Manipulating text and images
- Taking notes in digital ink
- Saving notes for review via e-mail, the Web, or print
- Viewing Web sites as a group
- Demonstrating concepts
- Creating digital lesson activities with templates and images
- Showing and writing notes over educational video sound bites
- Using presentation tools built into the interactive whiteboard to enhance learning materials

Other interesting ways that a whiteboard may be used is to write over video images and not only capture the video and notes, but also place multiple video images and annotations on a single page for comparison. You can integrate tools such as a graphing calculator, motion sensors, or concept-mapping software.

The whiteboard technology meets instructional needs by delivering the distance education lesson to students wherever they are located. When the "synpodium" is used, the instructor can use a touch-sensitive computer screen, rather than a large whiteboard, to accomplish the same instructional results. Research studies indicate that students are highly engaged when whiteboards are employed in instruction (Beeland, 2002). Research studies also indicate an increase in cognitive gain.

The Document Camera

The second form of media that may be used in distance education is the document camera. The projection system of the overhead projector, which is readily used in classroom instruction to project transparencies on a screen, cannot be used in a distance education configuration since the students are not present. The document camera is a television camera mounted downward on the display stage. The televised signal is transmitted through a switching device that transmits the signal to the students' computers.

A variety of visuals may be used on the document camera that will reinforce the performance objectives. These materials may be prepared using a computer word processor. The production principles of any instructional material are the same as those used to design a transparency:

- Allow a one-inch border around an 8½-by-11-inch piece of paper. Use a 24-point font that is easy to read.
- Limit the number of words to about six per line and limit each page to about six lines.
- Print the material on pastel paper. A light color background is more suitable for the camera and makes the text easier to read.

In addition to print media, graphics, illustrations, and other visuals are suitable for the document camera. Small objects such as calculators, measuring instruments, cross sections of plants, and the like, also referred to as manipulatives, that are small enough to fit on the stage, can be used to visually illustrate portions of the enabling objectives.

The document camera is probably used more for live or synchronous online courses than for asynchronous courses. However, arrangements can be made to use the document camera for an asynchronous course by recording various segments and placing them as video inserts into the instructional sequence.

PowerPoint and Macromedia Flash

Educational technologists at one time recommended the use of 35mm slide presentations to reinforce the terminal performance objective due to the visual nature of the medium. More sophisticated presentations could be accomplished by using an audio track as well as dual projectors that enabled the user to dissolve from one slide to another. Contemporary educational technologists, however, now advocate the use of PowerPoint and Macromedia Flash presentations, especially for online lessons.

PowerPoint and Macromedia Flash presentations can be thought of and developed as multimedia presentations. Individual slides can be produced using the traditional print media with an appropriate color background that enhances the visual presentation. In addition, all types of pictures, graphics, animation, and cartoons can be incorporated into the lesson to help students visualize the content. The use of PowerPoint also allows you to incorporate links to various Web sites for additional information. Downstreaming video may be used to show skills development as well as to visualize content. Audio may also be incorporated.

Additional Media

It should not be overlooked that additional instructional resources may be placed on a CD-ROM that becomes part of the distance-learning package for the student. The CD-ROM has a large capacity to manage quality audio, video, large quantities of text, graphics, photographs, animation, and so on.

The photo CD, or photographic compact disc, is a way for you to take your own photographs using a digital camera, store these images, and then transfer them onto your individual online lessons or to transfer them to a CD-ROM you have developed for your course.

The DVD-ROM (Smaldino et al., 2005) is another digital storage format that has greater capacity for storage. This format is ideal for large quantities of text, audio, and animation, as well as longer videos. The advantage of the DVD-ROM as a video format is that the viewer can decide how to interact with the material from a menu of choices.

SUMMARY

After completing the analysis and performance objective stages, you will need to select the content for the individual lesson. First, divide the terminal performance objective into subparts or enabling objectives. Second, search for lesson content that will reinforce the enabling objectives and in turn, reinforce the terminal performance objectives. Lesson content can be obtained by using various Internet search engines such as AltaVista, Yahoo, WebCrawler, and Google. Third, organize your content material using either a chronological, sequential, or topical order. Fourth, generate an outline and fill in the lesson with your lesson content. Fifth, design a summary to the lesson that reviews the performance objectives. Sixth, design an introduction that obtains student attention and serves as an advance organizer for the lesson.

Once the lesson has been designed, you will need to properly select appropriate instructional media that will reinforce the TPO. Students learn best by being directly involved in new content. Instructional media have several specific benefits:

- They create a direct substitute for the real learning experience.
- They create accurate communication.
- They create alternatives for learning.
- They create excitement and curiosity in learning.

Selection criteria should be used when incorporating instructional media into the lesson:

- Select instructional media that reinforces terminal performance objectives.
- Select instructional media that has accurate information.
- Select instructional media that engages the student.
- Select instructional media that is free from bias.
- Select instructional media that has good production quality.

There is great value in the use of visuals in the teaching/learning process. Visuals can translate the abstract, and sometimes very vague, concepts into understandable concepts. Visuals provide a concrete reference to abstract concepts.

A variety of instructional media are available to reinforce your performance objectives. Traditional forms of media, for example, the chalkboard, overhead projector, and slide projector, are not appropriate for online instruction lessons. However, each has been replaced with smarter technology. The blackboard has been replaced with the electronic whiteboard, the overhead projector has been replaced with the document camera, and the slide projector has been replaced with PowerPoint and Macromedia Flash. Other forms of technology may be used, such as CD-ROM, Photo CD, and DVD-ROM.

CASE STUDIES

Course Description No. 1

Course: BIOL 6000/8000 Introduction to Scientific Thought and Expression
Instructor: Dr. Earnest DuBrul, associate professor, biology
The teaching strategy used for this course is constructivist approach.

The 5 Es Approach

Each session progresses through the 5 Es: engage, explore, explain, elaborate, and evaluate. This instructional model was developed by Rodger Bybee and BSCS. The 5 Es are based on the assumption that adults, as well as

(continued)

(continued)

children, acquire knowledge by constructing it for themselves and building on what they already know. Teachers may find the 5 Es useful in their own teaching. Each of the sessions will contain activities that progress from *engage* to *evaluate*. As you progress through the sessions following the 5 Es, you will experience constructivist learning yourselves.

Engage: Initiates the learning tasks, makes connections between past and present learning experiences, and focuses thinking on the learning outcomes of the current activity.

Explore: Provides a common base of experiences within which the current concepts, processes, and skills are identified and developed.

Explain: Focuses attention on a particular aspect of the engage and explore experiences. Also provides opportunities for participants to develop explanations and for teachers to introduce concepts, processes, or skills.

Elaborate: Challenges and extends participants' conceptual understanding and skills. Through new experiences, participants develop a deeper and broader understanding, acquire more information, and refine skills.

Evaluate: Encourages participants to assess their understanding and abilities and provides opportunities for teachers to evaluate progress toward achieving learning outcomes.

(Adapted from Bybee, 1977)

An extended syllabus contains required readings, exercises, and videos for content reinforcement.

Course Description No. 2

Course: MET 3100 Applied Thermodynamics
Instructor: Dr. Ella Fridman, associate professor, engineering technology

Modules are completed with assigned text reading as well as online reading assignments. The reading assignments are reinforced by animations and demonstrations with embedded questions. A prompt may be used to check appropriate answers. Instructional media is used to reinforce both the diesel- and gasoline-powered engines by using motion models. After the student has completed the online reading and the animations/demonstrations, concept questions are to be answered and submitted for evaluation. A laboratory experiment is to be conducted concerning the approximate versus exact analysis of ideal gas cycles.

(continued)

(*continued*)

Course Description No. 3

Course: CIEC 3200 Philosophy and Practice in Early Childhood Education
Instructor: Dr. Bob Cryan, professor, early childhood education
Instructional content: Order instructional content, support material, design summary, design introduction, and select media

1. Students are assigned to read a required chapter in their textbook.
2. Students are to read the extended instructor's notes that detail very specific theories presented in reading assignment.
3. Students are then required to answer two questions posed by the instructor. Students are to discuss these questions in their small groups and then post their summary to these questions on the bulletin board under Small Groups Summary.
4. Other small groups are to read and respond to these summaries.

REFERENCES

Beeland, W. (2002). *Student engagement, visual learning and technology: Can interactive white boards help?* Accessed October 17, 2004, from http://chiron.valdonsta.edu/are/Artmanscript/vol1no1/beeland_am.pdf.

Bybee, R. (1977). *Achieving scientific literacy: From purposes to practices.* Portsmouth, NH: Heinemann.

Gagné, R. (1985). *The conditions of learning and theory of instruction.* (4th ed.). New York: Holt, Rinehart and Winston.

Harris, R. (2000). *A guidebook to the Web.* Guilford, CT: Dushkin/McGraw-Hill.

Koontz, F. R. (1996). *Media and technology in the classroom.* (5th ed.). Dubuque, IA: Kendall/Hunt.

Simonson, M., Smaldino, S., Albright, M., & Zvacek, S. (2003). *Teaching and learning at a distance: Foundations of distance education.* (2nd ed.). Upper Saddle River, NJ: Merrill/Prentice Hall.

Smaldino, S., Russell, J., Heinich, R., & Molenda, M. (2005). *Instructional technology and media for learning.* (8th ed.). Upper Saddle River, NJ: Pearson/Merrill/Prentice Hall.

Smart Technologies, Inc. (2004). Classroom case studies. Accessed from http://www.smarttech.com.

CHAPTER 7

Step 4: Implement Instruction

CHAPTER OUTLINE

Design an Extended Syllabus
Design Individual Sessions Into Modules
Module Design
Live Orientation Session
Summary
Case Studies
   Course Description No. 1
   Course Description No. 2
   Course Description No. 3
Reference

KNOWLEDGE OBJECTIVES

At the end of this chapter, you should be able to:

1. Justify the rationale for developing an extended syllabus.
2. Identify the basic essentials contained in an extended syllabus.
3. Defend the rationale for writing detailed instruction for course requirements.
4. Identify reasons for designing performance objectives for each chapter if they are not already contained in the textbook.
5. Justify the rationale for including a student information sheet in the extended syllabus.
6. Identify the purposes of a module.
7. Describe the reasoning to gain student attention as they study the module.
8. List the purposes of designing an advance organizer.
9. Describe the SQ3R method of reading.
10. Summarize the importance of engaging students in post-reading exercises.
11. Justify the use of a live orientation session for a distance-learning course.
12. Describe what should be reviewed during the live orientation session.
13. Justify the creation of a buddy system for students enrolled in an online course.

LEXICON

Terms to know:

advance organizer	implementation stage
buddy system	module
extended syllabus	SQ3R method

The first three steps of the ASSIST-Me model have now been completed. In step 1 you analyzed the course selection, curriculum, instructional setting, and students. In step 2 you developed performance objectives for the online lesson. In step 3 you selected the content for the online lesson, organized the content using an appropriate structure, and selected instructional media that reinforces the performance objectives.

The design of instruction phase is now complete. If you were to look at the entire outline of the ASSIST-Me model, you would be able to observe that the first three steps of the model deal with designing or creating the instruction. In step 4 you are going to implement or put this instruction into action.

DESIGN AN EXTENDED SYLLABUS

It is customary to write a syllabus for your classroom courses containing the traditional information: the name of the instructor, the text that will be used, objectives for the course, and reading assignments. This type of syllabus has traditionally been short, since you could clarify student questions in class. However, since a separation between you and your students exists in both time and space with distance learning, it is appropriate to design an extended or much more comprehensive syllabus that will give support to the student during the entire course. Here are the basic essentials that should be contained in the extended syllabus.

1. *Course title.* List the name of the course, day and time of meeting, as well as the semester and year.
2. *Instructor.* Indicate the instructor's name, rank, office number, office phone number, home phone number, cell phone number, and e-mail address. Indicate office hours and when students may make an appointment for a conference.
3. *Course description.* The approved course description may be found in the curriculum catalog. It is suggested that the course description be carefully analyzed for accuracy. Be sure the course goal is accurately stated. Repeat the course description in your syllabus.
4. *Course goals.* You may have a very general course goal for the entire course. However, this course goal can probably be broken into specific objectives for each of the online sessions. Write all of the course objectives using the 4 S method.

5. *Prerequisites.* List all prerequisite courses the student should have completed to gain admission to this course. Also include all pre-requisite skills the student should have to successfully complete this course.

6. *Standards.* Indicate the standards set forth by any national organization that this course meets.

7. *Course materials.* Indicate the required text(s), workbooks, lab manuals, and so forth for the course. You may also want to indicate texts for supplemental reading that will enrich the required text material.

8. *Objectives for each chapter.* If your text contains performance objectives for each chapter, indicate to the students that these should be carefully reviewed before reading the chapter. This will guide your students to look for the answers to these performance objectives. If the text does not provide these performance objectives, it is strongly suggested that you write out performance objectives for each chapter. These performance objectives will be the same objectives you have already written for each of the on-line lessons.

9. *Companion Web site.* You may wish to develop a companion Web site that describes the individual online lessons. This Web site may include a short introduction to the individual session and a risk-free quiz with immediate feedback that covers each of the performance objectives for the lesson. Additional material may be included, such as the lexicon of new vocabulary for the lesson, articles at various Web sites that you want students to read, as well as a summary of the lesson. It is up to you to creatively design the companion Web site and its use.

10. *Course requirements.* You will want to list all of the assignments and tests and the percentage each is worth for the course. For example, the midterm and final may be worth 40% of the grade. The course requirements should also indicate the chapters or online lessons each test will cover. The assignments, projects, and so on, are then worth 60% of the grade. Be as detailed as possible in this section.

11. *Description of course projects.* Here is where you may want to be much more detailed about the course requirements. Describe in detail each of these course projects. Give your students a description

of the projects, with specific direction as to how they will complete the objective. This description may also include the criteria you will use to grade the project. These criteria will also serve as a guideline and checklist for students to follow.

12. *Web sites.* You may want to give the students Web sites that will give them detailed information that will assist them to complete the assignment. Included in this section could also be journals, periodicals, and other texts.

13. *Grading system.* Be specific in your grading system. Explain what students need to do to earn an A, B, or C, and so forth.

14. *Course policies.* You will need to address several issues here. First, what is your course policy on due dates for assignments and taking tests? You will need to indicate what students must do if they become ill and cannot fulfill an assignment or an exam. Next, you will want to address the issue of academic dishonesty and state what the school's policy is on this issue. Third, address the policy on student disability and how the situation may be addressed. Finally, address the issue of copyright and your policy on copying assignments or illegally obtaining information from various Internet sources.

15. *Course calendar.* Indicate when sessions should be completed. This will assist the students, especially in an asynchronous course, to pace themselves in completing the course assignments. If the course is synchronous, indicate what session you will be covering each week.

16. *Student information.* It is vital for you to obtain specific information from your students, such as full name and any nickname, telephone number, e-mail address, major, minor, and so on. In addition, you will want to learn what knowledge and skills the students may already possess for the course. You may want to ask the students if they want to learn any particular knowledge or skills from your course. This helps you to learn more about the students' general characteristics, specific entry-level skills, as well as learning styles. This student information sheet may be online and students can complete it and e-mail it to you. You may also want to have a live general orientation for all of the students at the beginning of the course and have the students complete it at that time.

DESIGN INDIVIDUAL SESSIONS INTO MODULES

A module is best defined as a self-contained unit of instruction designed for the individual student. Each module will have standardized components, that is, the module may follow a template to be completed for the individual session.

At the beginning of each module, inform the students whether the performance objectives must be followed in a linear fashion or if they can be branched. If the performance objectives are to be followed in a linear manner, then the objectives must be followed in the designated sequence. In other words, performance objective 1 will be followed by 2, performance objective 2 will be followed by 3, and so on. If, however, the students may use the branching approach, that is, they may engage the performance objectives in any order, this control needs to be indicated to the student.

It is also suggested that the information be divided into smaller, manageable units of study ranging from approximately 10 to 30 minutes in length. Research studies indicate that small chunks of information are easier to master than very long segments (Carliner, 2002). This is partly due to the medium in which you are working. Students are accustomed to watching television in short segments followed by several commercials. This also carries over into learning new information. However, attention span is also dependent upon the educational and age maturity of the student. Undergraduate students have a slightly shorter attention span when it comes to comprehending new material. However, it has been found that nontraditional students as well as graduate students have more desire to learn new information and are more goal oriented. Slightly longer chunks of information may be designed for these students.

Customarily, you design your module around individual performance objectives for each of the sessions. However, you should identify those objectives that are comprehensive. These objectives may take longer than about 30 minutes to learn. This type of objective should be divided into two or three sessions.

For each module's performance objective, consider naming each of the segments. Though no standards or guidelines have been established, try to create a name for each of the objectives that will serve as a cue about that particular objective. For example, one of the objectives for this chapter is "Defend the rationale for writing detailed instruction for course requirements." This not only reflects content of the chapter, but also serves as an advance organizer for the reader.

MODULE DESIGN

There is no specific way in which a module should be developed. However, some basics should be included in each module to assist students in learning the new material.

1. *Gain student attention.* Never take for granted that the students are truly interested in your course or any of the sessions you have designed. When students first begin to study your module, you need to gain and focus their attention on the performance objectives and the importance of learning this content. Take for example, the introduction you read in chapter 5 concerning the designing of performance objectives. The historical account of the sinking of the *Bismarck* was used to gain your attention concerning the importance of including and properly designing performance objectives that will enable you to direct the design of the online lesson. Gaining the attention of the audience, or in this case, gaining the students' attention toward the lesson content, increases the likelihood that not only will they give greater attention to the lesson content, but the comprehension of the lesson content should also increase.

2. *Present the knowledge objectives.* If your textbook contains specific knowledge objectives for each chapter, direct the students to read these objectives carefully and to find the answers to these objectives during their reading. If, however, performance objectives have not been included in the chapter, you will need to carefully read this material and design performance objectives for your students. You must realize that your students do not have the skills to comprehensively read the content of a chapter and determine what the author had in mind for the objective. In fact, the author may be not that clear in his or her writing. If this is the case, it is even more important for you to design the objectives for your students.

3. *Design an advance organizer.* Research has proven that an advance organizer will improve comprehension. The advance organizer is an outline of the chapter to be read and directs the students' attention to the organization of and relationships between major topics. If the text does not provide an outline, then you will need to design an outline. The most simplistic advance organizer is nothing more than the major headings of the chapter. A more comprehensive advanced organizer would include subtopics.

4. *Introduce new terms.* The jargon used in any course will be new to the students. List new terms that will be contained in the assigned chapter and direct the students to learn the definitions.
5. *Present a risk-free quiz.* A good way to start students focusing on the new material is to offer a risk-free quiz to determine how much they may already know as well as what they do not know. For the most part, students like a challenge and are accustomed to taking tests. Risk-free quizzes, that is, quizzes that are not recorded as test scores and do not become part of the students' record for the course, have been found to be an interesting way to introduce the new subject content and gain students' attention. Students will need immediate feedback to this quiz. The key to the quiz may be included at the end of the module.
6. *Present the reading.* Direct the student to read the assignment by using the SQ3R method. For the most part, we make an assumption that students have good reading skills. This is not necessarily true. Most of us do not have really good reading skills.

The SQ3R method of reading is simple and stands for survey, question, read, recite, and review. What you are doing is to encourage the student to attack the chapter and be aggressive in finding the information.

First, students should survey the entire chapter. This includes reading the introduction, skimming the section titles, and reading the summary of the chapter. Then students must question what they are reading. Here is where students will want to refer to the performance objectives and begin to speculate as to what the answers may be. Then students will quickly read the chapter, but not for detail. When a term is not understood, students should make a simple check mark in the column or underline the word. If a concept is not understood, students should place a question mark in the side column. This is not the time to highlight or underline the text. When finished with this stage, students again begin to review what they have read. Again, they should refer to the performance objectives and attempt to answer these objectives. The last stage is to review the content of the chapter for complete comprehension. At this time, the students will highlight important concepts, underline the more important concepts, and make side notes in the chapter, all the while referring to the performance objectives. When finished, the student should be able to answer the performance objectives.

7. *Present a posttest.* Now that the students have completed the required reading, you may want to design a second, more comprehensive risk-free quiz. This is sometimes referred to as a posttest. The first risk-free quiz is a pretest. This test is also for practice and is not counted as a required test.

8. *Design exercises.* The purpose of any exercise is to engage the student in the lesson content. This may include drill-and-practice, gaming, simulations, discovery, problem solving, case studies, and the like. A complete discussion of these exercises will be included in the next chapter. Whatever exercise you design, the purpose is to immerse the students in the subject content to promote learning.

9. *Web site support.* It is extremely helpful to the student if Web sites where students may find answers and additional information to the performance objectives are presented. Not all answers may be found in the text you are using. This also may encourage you to create performance objectives that are outside the scope of the text.

LIVE ORIENTATION SESSION

For some students, limited access to the instructor remains a barrier to the concept of learning at a distance. The feeling of isolation, with limited or no interaction or feedback with the instructor as well as with other students, dampens the desire to take a course that stresses individual responsibility on the part of the student. Students who have not previously taken online courses have a major adjustment to make from the social atmosphere of the classroom to the isolated atmosphere of the computer in the student's room. If it is possible, a live orientation session at the beginning of the course may put some of these student concerns to rest.

For students who may have previously taken an online course, as well as those students who are taking their first online course, the live orientation session at the beginning of the course can solve much student anxiety.

The purpose of the live orientation session is to acquaint the students with the extended syllabus, the organization of the course, and especially how they can receive help and get into contact with you.

Start first with the extended syllabus. Remember to introduce yourself, the location of your office, telephone number, and especially your e-mail address. Review all the sections of the syllabus, especially the course goals, objectives, course requirements, and criteria for completing the assignments, as well as your grading system. Entertain questions from the class about the syllabus.

Second, introduce the modules into which the course is divided, what is included in each module, and deadlines for completing the modules. You will need to explain whether students will need to study each module in a particular order, that is, to study the performance objectives in the sequence they are presented, or they may randomly select performance objectives to study. You will want to encourage the student to take the pretests, read the assignments using the SQ3R method, take the posttests, and work with the provided exercises. You will need to encourage the students to use the links provided in each module.

Since this type of course stresses more student independence to learn the material, you may want to establish small study groups, sometimes referred to as the buddy system. Telephone numbers may be exchanged among students to establish these small study groups. Students will need to have the freedom to study independently or to join a support study group.

SUMMARY

Step 4, the implementation step, is the stage where you will give the designed instruction to the student. During steps 1, 2, and 3, you designed the course of study. Now you are ready to present and engage the student in a course of study.

Since you are separated in both time and space from the student, you will need to design an extended syllabus that is both comprehensive and detailed. It should contain the following essentials:

1. Course title
2. Name of the instructor, office telephone number, e-mail address, etc.
3. Course description
4. Course goals
5. Prerequisites
6. Standards to be met
7. Course materials
8. Objectives for each chapter
9. Companion Web site
10. Course requirements
11. Description of course projects

12. Web sites
13. Grading system
14. Course policies
15. Course calendar
16. Student information sheet

The implementation of courses content is presented in a modular format. A module is defined as a self-contained unit of instruction that follows, to some extent, a particular arrangement. Modules may be designed in the following format.

1. Gain student attention.
2. Present the knowledge objectives.
3. Design an advance organizer.
4. Introduce new terms.
5. Present a risk-free quiz as a pretest.
6. Present the reading introducing the SQ3R method.
7. Present a posttest.
8. Design exercises.
9. Offer Web site support.

When it is possible, it is highly recommended that a live orientation session be conducted. During this orientation session, you will want to review the extended syllabus and the modular design of the instruction for each of the sessions and encourage students to ask questions about the course. Finally, you may want to establish a buddy system where students can form small study groups.

CASE STUDIES

Course Description No. 1

Course: BIOL 6000/8000 Introduction to Scientific Thought and Expression
Instructor: Dr. Earnest DuBrul, associate professor, biology

An extended syllabus is posted along with detailed information for each module. Specific readings, as posted in the module, are assigned along with viewing

(continued)

(*continued*)

video segments that reinforce readings and provide information for posted questions. Answers are posted and shared with paired students.

Course Description No. 2

Course: MET 3100 Applied Thermodynamics
Instructor: Dr. Ella Fridman, associate professor, engineering technology

A syllabus is posted along with the course schedule. Each lesson is divided into a module complete with online reading assignments, animations and demonstrations, and concept questions.

Course Description No. 3

Course: CIEC 3200 Philosophy and Practice in Early Childhood Education
Instructor: Dr. Bob Cryan, professor, early childhood education

Design an extended syllabus
Design individual sessions into modules
Live orientation session

A detailed syllabus is posted with the name of the required text, explanation of posted lecture notes for each module, assignments, quizzes, questions to be answered by small groups, criteria for review of journal article, procedure for completing student reflective journal, the communication process that will be used for the course, and so on. A detailed welcome and introduction to the course is posted during the first week of class.

REFERENCE

Carliner, S. (2002). *Designing e-learning*. Alexandria, VA: ASTD.

CHAPTER 8

Step 5: Solicit Student Response to Instruction

CHAPTER OUTLINE

Scenario 1
Scenario 2
Scenario Evaluation
The Process of Engaging the Student
Meaningful Learning Through Problem Solving
Students Need to Learn to Problem Solve
A Problem Defined
Designing an Authentic Problem
Examples of Authentic Problems
Strategies for Solving Research-Type Problems
Problem Solving Beyond Research
The Role of the Faculty in Authentic Problem Solving
The Evaluation Process
Results
Summary
Scenario Analysis
Case Studies
    Course Description No. 1
    Course Description No. 2
    Course Description No. 3
References

KNOWLEDGE OBJECTIVES

At the end of this chapter, you should be able to:

1. Explain the process of engaging the students during an online lesson.
2. Define and give an example of an authentic and meaningful task.
3. Describe what meaningful learning through problem solving means.
4. Summarize the process of how students can learn to solve problems.
5. Explain the conditions of what constitutes a problem.
6. Describe the steps of designing an authentic problem.
7. Compare and contrast a defined and ill-defined problem.
8. Identify a strategy for solving an authentic problem.
9. Construct an authentic problem and create a hypothesis for the problem.
10. Describe the various types of problems that may be designed.
11. Summarize the role of the faculty in authentic problem solving.
12. Analyze which faculty role is more suitable for online teaching.
13. Explain the evaluation process of authentic problem solving.
14. Summarize the research results found using engagement theory.

(continued)

(continued)

LEXICON

Terms to know:

algorithmic problems	meaningful learning
authentic problem	problem
case study problems	problem analysis
design problems	qualitative measures
decision-making problems	quantitative measures
diagnosis-solution problems	rule-using problems
engagement theory	story problems
hypothesis	tactical/strategic problems
logical problems	troubleshooting problems

SCENARIO 1

A young, highly qualified professor was asked to teach an online course. He had received extremely high evaluations in his classroom teaching and students really enjoyed his classes and style of teaching. However, he had no experience teaching online courses. As he took his time to reevaluate his lecture style of teaching, he was very careful to check and correct his lecture notes for accuracy, his discussion questions, and assignments. He then transferred them to his online course.

The course seemed to be received well by the students, although many more students dropped his course than usual. However, the young professor also noticed that the average student grade was lower than in his classroom-based class.

At the end of the course, as was customary, the course was evaluated in the same fashion as the traditional classroom class. Much to the disappointment of the young professor, his teaching evaluation was much lower than his classroom teaching evaluations. Many students were very disappointed about their online experience and made several negative statements.

- "I was highly disappointed in this course. The computer became a glorified page-turner for the lectures. I became bored with just reading the assignments, then answering the questions, completing the assignments, and then taking a test. I'm never going to take another online course. They are a waste of my time."
- "I was really confused as to what the professor wanted me to do with the questions. I read all the material but the questions did not make any sense. I did not know how to answer the questions."

- "I really missed discussing the material that I read. When I was in the classroom, I could ask questions or join in a class discussion about the subject content. I could ask the professor for clarification. I really felt isolated and had no one to talk to."

SCENARIO 2

A very experienced and successful professor, who had taught online courses for several years and had received very high student evaluations, decided to energize his course. His goal was to have the students learn more in his course. After doing some reading about engaging students in problem-based learning, he decided to make some changes to his course. He began to introduce very complex, ill-defined problems for the students to solve for each of the chapters. Each problem was to be analyzed and a solution for the problem was to be submitted at the end of each session before the student could start the next chapter.

As the course progressed, the experienced professor noticed that it was taking the students much longer to complete the chapter problems. He also began to receive a rash of e-mail messages concerning how the students were to solve the problems, where to get the necessary information, and what was the expected outcome of the assignments. There were multiple solutions for each of the problems; which one was correct?

As it was customary, the professor had his online course evaluated. He was shocked to learn that the students did not like this way of learning. Some of the comments received by the professor were disconcerting.

- "This course is not what I expected. In other courses that you have taught you gave us the information that was needed and then asked some questions about the content. In this course you did not give us any direction as to how you expected us to solve the problems you gave us. Some of us worked together but it did not seem to help. Some of the students really got into some bitter arguments over how to solve the problem."
- "The problems you gave us were very challenging. They seemed fun at first but then I ran out of time. The problems became too difficult for me to handle. I became confused as to which answer to use. You needed to give us more direction."
- "At first I accepted the challenge of answering what you called ill-defined problems. I know that you were giving us a challenge but I

was not really prepared for this type of a challenge. The more I read the more I got confused. None of the information I got seemed to really answer the questions. That was another problem. I didn't fully understand the problem and how to solve it. I need more help!"

SCENARIO EVALUATION

After reading these two case studies that involve teaching online courses and after reading this chapter, you should conduct an analysis of the problems presented in each of the scenarios by using the ASSIST-Me model and information found in this chapter.

Several questions need to be addressed:

1. What caused the negative student reactions?
2. What caused students to not want to take another online course in scenario 1?
3. What caused students to drop the course in scenario 2?
4. What should have been done to prevent these problems?

THE PROCESS OF ENGAGING THE STUDENT

Instructional design models are based on learning theory for students to learn in the traditional environment of the classroom, where the instructor can monitor student behavior, guide student learning, and answer questions. Customarily, it was thought that students would be engaged in learning more on an individual basis: student with content, student with student, and student with teacher. Although ID models can be applied to the context of online learning situations, the lack of instructional strategies for expanded student engagement for online courses needs to be addressed.

Engagement theory requires that students must be purposefully engaged in authentic tasks in meaningful ways for learning to occur (Kearsley & Schneiderman, 1998). This also implies that students should be highly engaged in activities that involve cognitive processes such as creating, problem solving, reasoning, decision making, and evaluation.

Engagement theory involves three major characteristics: it is collaborative, problem based, and authentic (Kearsley, 2000). Collaborative means that students must co-labor or work together as a team to ascertain pertinent information and work among teachers, subject matter experts (SMEs), and so forth, to determine the necessary information that would lead to possible solutions to the authentic problem. Problem based, as implied in engagement theory, means student activities involve completing assignments and projects rather than taking tests. Finally, authentic means the problems presented are as realistic as possible and directed toward the needs and interests of students. Students also may be required to define a project of their own interest, thereby having a sense of control over their learning, which is absent in the traditional classroom environment.

MEANINGFUL LEARNING THROUGH PROBLEM SOLVING

Learning is driven by the type of task to be performed (Jonassen et al., 2003). Taking a test requires ordering and memorizing information to satisfy a test question. Writing a term paper requires the acquisition of information, creation of a thesis statement, organization of the information into some logical sequence, and the offering of some type of conclusion. Writing also includes the use of rules of grammar and sentence construction. The type of task the students perform determines the type of learning. In order to have a meaningful learning experience, the students must be engaged in a meaningful learning task. The goal of engagement should require students to participate in active, constructive, intentional, authentic, and cooperative learning activities (Jonassen et al., 2003).

We solve problems on a daily basis, from the time we start the working day until the end of the day. We are constantly engaged in solving problems, from the very small problem of calculating how much time it will take us to arrive on time to a business meeting, to major problems that require a copious amount of time, resources, and personnel. When we are solving problems in these situations, we are experiencing meaningful learning because the task is meaningful. To solve the problem, the problem must be defined and a suitable solution must be employed. If the incorrect solution is applied to the problem, learning will still occur. We have learned what does not work. We must redefine the problem and apply a more appropriate solution. This problem-solving cycle continues until the correct solution is found.

Solving given problems, from the very simple to the most complex, is meaningful learning. Problem solving can be a meaningful form of learning in our formal educational settings (Jonassen et al., 2003). The purpose of formal education should be to develop problem-solving skills, not memorizing facts. Most students will spend the greater part of their time in an out-of-school environment. Learning to take a test does not create problem solvers. Learning techniques to solve problems does develop problem solvers.

STUDENTS NEED TO LEARN TO PROBLEM SOLVE

Traditionally, students are accustomed to a passive learning environment where the instructor has the students read a required chapter in the course textbook, then delivers a lecture with elaboration as to what the students have read. The students are then assigned to perform a task that gives them some type of transfer of information. Finally, the students are tested for knowledge gain. In this environment, the students are given explicit direction as to what they are to do, how they are to perform the task, and when it must be completed. The students are not required to make decisions about their own learning, but rather to follow directions. Obviously, these students, at this point of their education, do not possess problem-solving skills since they have not yet been taught or even had the opportunity to solve authentic problems. Due to this long and engrained teaching/learning tradition, the introduction of engagement theory should be done on a graduated scale.

Students need to learn how to learn online, especially when they will be engaged in their own learning. This is a new environment and a new way of learning. It is necessary that you conduct a "learn how to learn" session to orient the students (Lim, 2004). You may want to start with a very simple project of having students becoming acquainted with one another. Having students create a biography as well as having them state their expectations of the course may accomplish this. Then the students must post this in a discussion forum. Each student should be given the responsibility to read the biographies and course goals of the other students. An online discussion follows, facilitated by the instructor, dealing with the students' background skills as well as what they expect from the course.

From this getting-acquainted stage, you can then assign students to work in pairs or small groups, with similar expectations and backgrounds, on a simple problem that has a defined solution. The students should be given more direction as to how to solve the task and where they may find specific information that will assist in solving the problem. Once the students believe they have solved the problem, the answer should be posted and defended with the reasons why the group thinks it is the correct answer. The groups could then compare and critique answers and discuss the information they obtained and how they arrived at their answers.

A PROBLEM DEFINED

A problem needs at least two conditions. First, when the solution to a question is unknown, it becomes a problem. Second, a situation becomes a problem when there is value in the solution. The problem must have some intellectual, social, or cultural worth. If you do not believe it is worth the time and effort to seek the solution, the situation is not perceived as a problem.

DESIGNING AN AUTHENTIC PROBLEM

You will note that the first problem the students encountered was labeled as a simple problem that had a single solution. A simple problem is well defined, clearly stated, and has only a single answer that can be verified by the information obtained. All of the teams had the same problem and then had the opportunity to collaborate on their solutions. This created a common experience where the process of obtaining the information could be shared and solutions could be compared for correctness. However, authentic problems that elicit meaningful learning that can be transferred to other learning situations must be carefully written and follow some specific guidelines.

First, the authentic problem is ill-defined, having no single answer and multiple ways to arrive at the solution. The problem must contain many variables that must be individually addressed. Each proposed solution, if implemented, must be carefully analyzed as to its probability of working. Its advantages, disadvantages, and "what could go wrong" scenarios must be carefully evaluated. A true authentic problem most closely approximates a real-world situation.

Second, the problem should be relevant to the student to create and sustain interest. The problem-solving process probably will take slightly longer than either the student or you have anticipated. To assist in creating authentic problems, the students may also be asked to submit authentic problems that would be of interest to them. This gives the students practical experience in identifying as well as describing the problem. The description of the problem should identify a major concept or main idea that should be investigated. The description should also include some explanation of what other researchers have found as well as information contained in related literature. Information about how and where to obtain necessary data that will assist in solving the problem should be included in the statement of the problem. Finally, the description should include how the data may be analyzed. The instructor may want the student teams to submit more than one problem for evaluation. Then, upon mutual agreement, the student team can select the one problem that is most appealing and interesting.

Third, the problem must have both limitations and delimitations. The problem must be limited in scope and should be able to be solved in a reasonable amount of time during the course. The students should be given some type of timetable for completion. For example, the students could be informed as to approximately how long it should take to analyze the problem, how much time should be spent in gathering related information and data, and how long it should take to analyze the data and come to some conclusion.

Fourth, in order to solve the problem, data must be able to be found or obtained. If data is not available, the problem cannot be solved.

Fifth, there should be sufficient related literature available for the student teams to obtain and evaluate. Hopefully, a landmark study or article can be found that will help the student teams to locate additional information as well as guidance in solving the authentic problem.

EXAMPLES OF AUTHENTIC PROBLEMS

One of the biggest tasks of engagement is the actual selection and writing of the authentic problem. Depending upon the discipline you are teaching, examples may take on a variety of subjects and levels of complexity. For example, one professor had students work on related campus projects such as developing an online system to schedule bus services, designing methods to maintain records for various recreational clubs, organizing car pools, and creating an accounting system for a department on campus (Kearsley & Shneiderman, 1999). Off-campus projects included donor and volunteer list management for a large charity, scheduling for a county recreation office, and information for a day care center. Other authentic problems included employee orientation programs, community outreach efforts, and alternative methods of training.

Another professor was more interested in and oriented toward research conducted in the area of engagement theory for his graduate class (Kearsley & Shneiderman, 1999). He had his students explore research topics.

- In which disciplines is engagement theory most or least effective?
- What skills do students need to effectively solve authentic problems?
- In what ways can individual differences be managed in collaborative work?
- What type of student evaluation methods are appropriate for authentic problem solving?
- In what way can the process of authentic problem solving be transferred to other types of learning?

STRATEGIES FOR SOLVING RESEARCH-TYPE PROBLEMS

As a consultant, you may want to give your students some vary basic problem-solving strategies to get them started. Here are some specifics that should give them some assistance.

1. *Analyze the problem.* After the students are teamed into small groups, they should be cautioned to carefully analyze and define the problem. Detailed and careful front-end analysis is crucial in defining the problem, as well as to the process of gathering related literature and research studies. An incorrect analysis of the problem will lead to incorrect answers to the problem. You may need to direct or coach the students to locate landmark papers and research studies that will provide a basis for their inquiry.

   It will be helpful for the students to begin identifying what is known and what is unknown about the problem as they conduct their literature search. Identifying what is known about the problem requires the students to use some Internet search strategies and obtain background information and related research studies. Once a sufficient amount of information is gathered, the students should group these judgments into areas of agreement, disagreement, and neutral positions. The result of this positioning may identify what is unknown and subsequently, what the problem to be solved is.

2. *State a hypothesis.* After the thorough analysis of the problem has been completed, a hypothesis may be created by the group. A hy-

pothesis is an inference made from what is known. It is an informed guess as to what the group believes the solution may be, based on the information they have obtained from their literature reviews.

3. *Test the hypothesis.* Hypothesis testing requires the students to obtain some type of evidence or data. It may have to be original data since the statement of the problem at this point has no answer. The groups may design special research-gathering instruments to obtain this data or search-related research studies that contain related research-gathering tools.

4. *Analyze the data.* Once the data has been obtained, it must be tested. An appropriate statistical analysis must be used for the data. Once the data analysis has been completed, the results may be applied to the hypothesis.

5. *State the conclusion.* The hypothesis may then be accepted or rejected depending upon the findings. The conclusion drawn from the data is the proposed solution, that is, the hypothesis. It is either correct or not correct. If it is not correct, the group must go back to the hypothesis stage and revise it for another possible solution. This process is cyclical until the best solution to the problem is discovered. If it is correct, then the hypothesis may be accepted.

6. *Recommendations.* From the acceptance of the hypothesis, the group must make some type of recommendation concerning its findings. These recommendations should also include how to implement the findings.

PROBLEM SOLVING BEYOND RESEARCH

A typology exists that offers a variety of different types of problems that evokes different forms of problem-solving skills (Jonassen et al., 2003). The range is from those problems that are well-defined, with a single method to solve the problem with a single solution, to those that are totally ill-defined and have multiple paths to multiple solutions.

You will recall that a well-defined problem presents all elements of the problem. It can be defined with a high degree of certainty. It has a limited number of rules and principles in a predictive and prescribed solution process and contains correct answers. At the other end of the continuum, ill-structured or ill-defined problems are defined with a great deal of uncertainty. The methodology used to solve such problems will have multiple paths. Once the solution has been found, it cannot be certain that it is the correct solution until it is tested in a real situation. Solutions to these ill-defined problems may, at times, be a best guess or personal opinion.

The typology presented begins with examples of simple types of problems and progresses to the more complex problems (Jonassen et al., 2003). Each presents a variety of variables to consider when seeking a correct or reasonable answer.

1. *Logical problems.* To solve logical problems, students must determine a specific method of reasoning that will yield an appropriate solution. The use of deductive and inductive reasoning is employed. Problems of this nature are used to sharpen mental acuity, clarity, and reasoning skills.

2. *Algorithmic problems.* These problems are commonly found in courses of mathematics and science. Students are taught to solve problems using formulas that yield an answer. Related courses in statistics also use this principle when calculating if there is a significant difference between the scores of two identically taught courses. Other examples can range from solving particular mathematic calculations to the amount of ingredients needed for a 12-inch double-layer chocolate cake in a home economics class. Algorithmic problems are also solved in assembling prefabricated furniture and even when using a computer program.

3. *Story problems.* One of the most common and easy to design, the story problem is found in all levels of education. The story problem narrative contains essential elements that must be considered to solve the problem. To be successful in solving the story problem, the learner must be able to accurately identify the structure of the problem. Once completed, the learner then selects the most appropriate formula for solving the problem. The values in the story problem are extracted and then inserted into the formula. Following the steps of the formula, the learner finds the solution to the story problem.

4. *Rule-using problems.* This type of problem recalls previously learned rules and applies them to new situations. It may be as simple as setting a formal table for a gourmet meal, to computing a corporate income tax return. Using search strategies on the Internet to locate needed information is also a good example. Here the search strategies range from the simple, as in using a single descriptor to locate information, to the more complex strategy of using Boolean

logic. The outcome may be uncertain at times, depending upon the rules that are applied in problem-solving strategy.

5. *Decision-making problems.* From a list of choices, the student makes an informed decision to select a single answer. The informed choice comes from careful analysis of the choices. Each choice is examined as to its advantages, disadvantages, and alternatives. A practical example of this could be the type of computer to be selected, the best type of operating system to be used, and the type of software program that most closely meets the needs of the student.

6. *Troubleshooting problems.* The main purpose of troubleshooting is to diagnose a problem in a system and fix it. This type of problem solving requires previously learned knowledge of a system as well as a cause-and-effect relationship between the fault and repair methods. A hypothesis or best guess of the problem is developed and, by using various testing methods, the diagnosis is made and the problem repaired. This author has observed several television engineers setting up waveform monitors and attaching the leads to a television camera to diagnose a faulty system. When we take our car to the dealership, the mechanic hooks up various diagnostic instruments to determine why our car is not performing as it should, then replaces a faulty part with a new part. In each case, a specific procedure that has been previously learned is prescribed to locate the problem.

7. *Diagnosis-solution problems.* Diagnosis-solution is similar to troubleshooting, but may have multiple paths to reach a solution to the problem. When we are ill, we consult with a physician for a remedy for the illness. The doctor first looks at our present symptoms and has laboratory tests conducted. From the symptoms observed and the results of our laboratory tests, the doctor makes a diagnosis concerning the type of illness we have and then prescribes a medication or treatment to eliminate our illness.

8. *Tactical/strategic problems.* Thanks to our military, we civilians now have many improved ways we can solve problems that require a high level of technology. The popular History Channel television series *Tactical to Practical* regularly demonstrates what the military of the United States has had developed to equip our forces. The Global Positioning System, for example, a satellite triangulation tracking system to locate ground troops and ships initially developed for the military, can now be purchased and used by civilians

to use when they are hiking, hunting, sailing, and so on. Yet another form of tactical/strategic problem solving occurs when a company or institution is concerned as to what its goals and objectives will be in five or ten years and wishes to develop a strategy to accomplish those goals and objectives. This type of strategy formation is obtained from a system analysis or a design. Both tactics and strategy are used, for example, when a union and management are negotiating a new contract. Both contract teams construct various strategies to obtain what they want in the contract.

9. *Case study problems.* One of the most common types of problems to solve is the case study. It requires an understanding of multifaceted situations and system analysis. A very careful investigation of all facts, inferences, and variables is needed. Because of case study ambiguity, it is difficult to design methods to obtain information and methods to solve the problem. These problems tend to be highly ill-structured and solutions tend to be uncertain. At times, solutions may only be opinions backed by logic.

10. *Design problems.* One of the most ill-structured problems is the design of something. Designing requires a lot of subject matter knowledge and system design knowledge. Designing instruction for an online course is a design problem. Although the ASSIST-Me model may be followed, a multiple number of steps and methods can be used for each step to solve the design needs of an online course. Once the design has been completed, it must be formally tested to determine whether the design strategies are satisfactory for meaningful learning.

THE ROLE OF THE FACULTY IN AUTHENTIC PROBLEM SOLVING

To some extent, the teacher and student roles have changed. The role of the teacher has become more like that of a coach or a consultant. Some refer to this process as switching from the sage on the stage to the guide on the side (Smaldino et al., 2005). The teacher is no longer the wise, all-knowing professor who dispenses information to the students, but rather a guide who assists the students when they are in need of direction.

As a guide on the side, you will need to give your students initial guidance on either a problem that you have designed for them to solve or a problem that they have selected or designed on their own. In the first case, students may need some assistance as to how to define the statement of the problem and the necessary literature or antidotal evidence needed. In the latter case, you will need to carefully guide the students through the process of limiting their topic into a manageable problem that can be completed in a reasonable period of time. Defining and limiting the topic process is in itself a learning process.

As a guide on the side, you will also need to give your students positive feedback and encouragement as they travel through the process of solving the problem. Frustration is inevitable as they begin the process of attempting to clarify the problem. For the majority of students, this may be their first time attempting to solve a problem of major proportions that may have actual consequences. The students will also continue to be frustrated concerning the time it takes to complete the process. Again, the majority of students have never had to solve a problem that may take more than a few hours or even a few days. Frustration also occurs when it comes time to draw a conclusion based on the data collected. Making decisions or conclusions based on an ill-defined problem, creating a hypothesis on an unknown, and gathering and analyzing information that may not be the most pertinent and reliable will all lead to frustration and uneasiness.

The students' role has also changed, from passively reading the assignments, listening to a lecture, completing practice assignments, and taking a test that gives proof of knowledge gained, to taking charge of their own learning by solving authentic problems. The students can no longer rely on the instructor to give them complete direction, but must become more self-reliant in defining a problem, proposing a solution to the problem, and getting information that will either prove or disprove the proposed solution.

THE EVALUATION PROCESS

The process of measuring learning and determining the best way to measure learning is quite frustrating for both the instructor and the students. The range of quantitative and qualitative measurement strategies and skills varies greatly from one instructor to another.

Historically, emphasis was on quantitative measures such as achievement, ability, or intelligence tests (Kearsley, 2000). Later, a shift occurred more toward competency-based, qualitative assessment methods. Then portfolios became increasingly popular to assess learning in lieu of tests. In business and industry, performance-based methods of evaluation became common.

Evidently, the traditional method of learning emphasized an orderly accumulation of new knowledge, skills, and attitudes, as directed by performance objectives and tested in the traditional method of answering questions that provided evidence that the SKAs had been learned. However, this very neat and orderly traditional way of testing a student does not accurately measure a student's learning when the student is engaged in authentic problem solving. *The task of evaluating the knowledge of a student who has answered or proposed an answer to the authentic problem, however, must be evaluated in a manner that reflects process used to solve the problem.*

The evaluation process, and not specific knowledge of a subject, also presents an authentic problem to the instructor: What is the most appropriate way to evaluate the student? Designing specific criteria that accurately evaluates the answer given to the authentic problem would be nearly impossible. For the ill-designed problem, there may be no one answer, and only a best answer may be offered and defended by pure logic based on what anecdotal evidence may have been obtained.

The student group and individual students may be evaluated by designing a qualitative assessment that evaluates the process used to solve the authentic problem and not the solution itself.

- First, how well was the authentic problem defined? Was there an appropriate literature search conducted using the Internet that produced needed background information? Were seminal studies found that supported the statement of the problem?
- Second, how accurate was the statement of the problem? Was the statement of the problem clearly stated? Were parameters of the problem accurately described, i.e., the boundaries of what would be considered in solving the problem?
- Third, how well was the hypothesis stated? Did the hypothesis reflect the data obtained?
- Fourth, what type and quality of evidence and data was obtained? Did it provide evidence that could be analyzed? Did the data help the support of the answer? Was the data analyzed appropriately?
- Fifth, does the solution appear to be the best answer? Is the answer logical in respect to the data collected and the analysis of the data?

- Sixth, if the group had to reanalyze and evaluate the authentic problem again, what changes would they make in their process?

The goal of authentic learning by problem solving is that the learners are creating knowledge for themselves. The role of the instructor is to facilitate that goal. That being the case, another way of assessing student learning is to have the students evaluate themselves and the process used to evaluate the authentic problem. What types of problems did they encounter and how did they solve these problems? How could they have improved the process used to solve the authentic problem? Finally, if they had to do it all over again, what major changes would they make in their problem-solving process?

RESULTS

It is not difficult to conclude that this type of learning is more interesting and engaging, especially if the problems are relevant to the student (Gurrie, 2003). Research has shown that students who are engaged in problem-based learning have a more positive attitude toward their coursework (Jones, 1996). Courses in which students are engaged in problem solving also exhibit a higher retention rate.

Although the amount of research specifically focused on engagement theory is limited, the research that has been completed is both positive and encouraging. When conventional courses were compared to online courses that contain a high amount of engagement, research studies have concluded that students who are highly engaged do as well as their counterparts from the traditional classrooms on national exams (Levine, 2001). Research studies also have concluded that these students are better practitioners of their professions. Students acquire the necessary course knowledge and become proficient in problem solving, self-directed learning, and team participation.

SUMMARY

Engagement theory requires that students be purposefully engaged in authentic tasks in meaningful ways for learning to occur. The authentic problems are as realistic as possible and directed toward the needs and interest of the students. Activities involve completing assignments and projects with limited or no test taking.

Students must first be trained in the process of problem solving. After the students become acquainted, they may be divided into groups and given a simple problem that has a defined solution. The students should be given direction as to how to solve the task. The results should then be posted for all of the students to observe the answer and how it was derived. From this modest beginning of solving problems, ill-defined problems may be introduced that are not clearly defined, have multiple paths to solve the problem, and do not have abundantly clear answers. The students should be given information as to the process of solving the problem: analyzing and defining the problem, stating a hypothesis, testing the hypothesis by gathering data, analyzing the data, and drawing a conclusion.

The design of an authentic problem must follow some guidelines. First, the ill-defined problem must be rather vague, have multiple paths to achieve the solution, and may have multiple solutions. Second, the problem should be relevant to the student to create and sustain interest. Third, the problem must have limitations. The problem must be limited in scope and should be able to be solved in a reasonable amount of time during the course. Fourth, in order to solve the problem, data must be able to be found or obtained. If data is not available, the problem cannot be solved. Fifth, there should be sufficient related literature available for the student teams to obtain and evaluate. Hopefully, a landmark study or article could be found that would help the student teams to locate additional information as well as guidance in solving the authentic problem.

There exists a typology, designed by Jonassen et al. (2003), that contains a variety of problems that evoke different forms of problem-solving skills and ranges from the simple, well-defined problem to the complex, ill-defined problem. The examples contained in this group are logical, algorithmic, story, rule-using, decision-making, troubleshooting, diagnosis-solution, tactical/strategic, case study, and design problems.

The role of the faculty in the process of authentic problem-solving activities is one of a coach, a consultant, and a guide on the side. As a guide on the side, you need to give your students initial guidance on the problem selected and continual positive feedback and encouragement during the time it takes to solve the problem.

The role of the student has changed as well. The role of students has changed from passively reading the assignments, listening to a lecture, completing practice assignments, and taking a test that gives proof of knowledge gained, to taking charge of their own learning by solving authentic problems. The students can no longer rely on the instructor to give them complete direction but they can become more self-reliant in defining a problem, getting information that will either prove or disprove the proposed solution, and then proposing a solution.

The process of measuring learning and determining the best way to measure learning that has taken place in problem-based learning can be frustrating for both the instructor and the student. The task of evaluating knowledge of a student who has answered or proposed an answer to the authentic problem, however, must be evaluated in the manner that reflects the process used to solve the problem. Ill-defined, authentic problems may have no answer and the answer offered may be defended by logic based on anecdotal evidence obtained. Therefore, it is the process used by the student in obtaining the solution that must be examined, in other words, how well the problem was defined, the accuracy of the hypothesis, the type and quality of data gathered, the analysis used in examining the data, and the proposed solution to the problem.

Results of using engaging students in authentic problem solving are positive. Research shows that students who are highly engaged in online courses learn as much as students who are in the classroom. The online students are proven to be better problem solvers. Student attitudes are positive. An increase in retention rates of those courses where students are engaged is also noted.

SCENARIO ANALYSIS

These two scenarios exemplify two extremes of engaging students in an online course. In scenario 1, the professor uses the traditional lecture style of teaching. The students are comfortable in receiving the information from the professor whose role it is to be the "sage on the stage" and not having the students work to get the new information. The professor is the one who possesses the knowledge and dispenses this knowledge as it is needed by the students. The students, in turn, play the traditional passive role and like the traditional way of teaching: read the new information textbook, listen to a lecture by the professor about the readings, ask questions and participate in a class discussion, complete an assignment about the new information, and then take a test.

The students in this online course found themselves in a much different teaching/learning situation than they had previously experienced. They received the information, but the interactivity of the classroom was not available. Students did not have the opportunity to participate in class and ask questions about the readings, lectures, or assignments. They were required to complete assignments independently with much less feedback.

In summary, this first scenario illustrates a classic lecture teaching/learning phenomenon: the students read the assignment, read the lecture, complete an assignment, and then take a test. No student engagement with other students or the instructor is indicated. Assignments were not sufficiently clear to the students. You can understand why the students did not like this course and did not learn as much as the students who took this course in the traditional classroom.

In scenario 2, we find a much different case. The students found themselves in a very high-technology atmosphere with a high level of engagement in the subject content. In this case, we see an extreme amount of engagement, to the extent that the students are overwhelmed with the ill-defined problems that they have to solve. The experienced professor overlooks the fact that the students do not have the necessary problem-solving skills. The students have never been taught how to define a problem, construct a hypothesis, gather the necessary data to solve the problem, analyze the data, and then state a possible solution to the problem. In addition, the professor does not analyze the skills and time it takes to obtain the necessary information to solve the problem. Students do not have collaboration skills for solving problems. The expectations of the assignment are not made clear. No evaluation criteria are given to the students.

CASE STUDIES

Course Description No. 1

Course: BIOL 6000/8000 Introduction to Scientific Thought and Expression
Instructor: Dr. Earnest DuBrul, associate professor, biology

For this course, students are required to:

1. Complete session exercises and short essays related to Web assignments and text reading.
2. Participate in discussion postings.
3. Complete three projects.

(continued)

(*continued*)

   a. A personal reflection paper (6–8 pages) on your teaching about the nature of science and the difficulties or major questions you have encountered.
   b. A critical book review of 6–8 pages.
   c. Pair journaling of a book. Students participating in this project will pair with another student. As the pair of students reads a selected book, they will periodically post their ideas. Each pair member will read and respond to the postings of the other pair member. There must be a minimum of six postings and six responses by each member of the pair for a minimum of 2,500 words.

Course Description No. 2

Course: MET 3100 Applied Thermodynamics
Instructor: Dr. Ella Fridman, associate professor, engineering technology

The student is engaged in running an authentic laboratory problem experiment of approximate versus exact analysis of ideal gas cycles. Students are assigned into teams to work on the experiment and then to submit reports.

Course Description No. 3

Course: CIEC 3200 Philosophy and Practice in Early Childhood Education
Instructor: Dr. Bob Cryan, professor, early childhood education

Students are required to write their own student profile during the first week of class and then post it on the discussion bulletin board. All students are then to read each other's profiles and get acquainted.

    There are specific modules during the semester in which students are engaged in a problem-solving process. The chapter 4 module, for example, has two defined problems to be analyzed. Students are assigned into small groups to answer these questions. Once completed, the answers are posted on the bulletin board for other small groups to read and critique.

REFERENCES

Gurrie, J. (2003). *What's your problem? Increasing student motivation and quality of participation in discussions through problem-based learning.* Elearnspace. Retrieved November 5, 2004, from http://elearnspace.org/Articles/contributor/pbl.htm.

Jonassen, D., Howland, J., Moore, J., & Marra, R. (2003). *Learning to solve problems with technology: A constructivist perspective*. (2nd ed.). Upper Saddle River, NJ: Merrill.

Kearsley, G. & Shneiderman, B. (1999). *Engagement theory: A framework for technology-based teaching and learning*. Retrieved November 3, 2004, from http://home.sprynet.com/~gkearsley/engage.htm.

Kearsley, G. (2000). *Online education: Learning and teaching in cyberspace*. Stamford, CT: Wadsworth Thomson Learning.

Levine, A. (2001). *A PBL overview*. Retrieved November 5, 2004, from http://www.mcli.dist.maricopa.edu/pbl/info.html.

Lim, C. (2004, July/August). Engaging learners in online learning environments. *Tech Trends*, 16–23.

Smaldino, S., Russell, J., Heinich, R., & Molenda, M. (2005). *Instructional technology and media for learning*. (8th ed.). Upper Saddle River, NJ: Pearson/Merrill/Prentice Hall.

Step 6: Test, Evaluate, and Revise Instruction

PERFORMANCE OBJECTIVES

At the end of this chapter, you should be able to:

1. Explain the process of evaluation.
2. Define the need to develop an organized, systematic process of evaluation.
3. Explain when the process of evaluation should not be conducted.
4. Explain when the process of evaluation should be conducted.
5. Describe the primary purpose of evaluation.
6. Compare and contrast formative and summative evaluation.
7. Explain the process of conducting formative evaluation.
8. Explain the process of conducting summative evaluation.
9. Describe the traditional approach to summative evaluation.

(*continued*)

(*continued*)

10. Define level 1 evaluation.
11. Discuss the disadvantages of level 1 evaluation.
12. Discuss the process of using a model approach for summative evaluation.
13. Compare and contrast the advantages and disadvantages of conducting summative evaluation using the online instructor with an outside evaluator.

LEXICON

Terms to know:

evaluation as a process	informal formative evaluation
formal formative evaluation	level 1 evaluation
formative evaluation	summative evaluation

SCENARIO

An experienced associate professor was quite pleased with the instructional design of his course. He had very carefully written the goals for the course as well as the specific performance objectives for his individual sessions. He had developed assignments that would give students practical experience in applying what they had read and class discussions using the chat room technique. A very lengthy and involved project was assigned near the end of the course that would be a culminating experience where the students had to apply nearly everything learned in the class. The course included only brief midterm and final exams due to the culminating experience assignment.

At the completion of the course, the professor administered a traditional course evaluation survey that was used by the entire department. The survey covered items of knowledge of the field, the degree to which the professor was prepared for the individual sessions, course activities, the attitude of the professor toward the students, and so on. The last part of the evaluation included written student responses covering their likes and dislikes about the course and a question that dealt with how the course could be improved.

After the surveys had been statistically analyzed and mean scores with degrees of freedom had been determined, the professor was disappointed in the results. The survey did not tell him how well the students were learning the required performance objectives or the amount of time it took to complete their assignments, nor did it indicate specific attitudes of the students toward the activities in the course. The answers to the questions at the end of the survey did not reveal substantial information pertaining to any course changes that should be made.

What evaluation process would you suggest that would improve this course evaluation to obtain useful information to make informed decisions about redesigning the instruction of the course (1) for the improvement of learning, (2) to enable students to learn more efficiently, and (3) to obtain specific student attitudes toward the course?

EVALUATION AS A PROCESS

Generally, the first thought an instructor has when the term *test* is used is the process of evaluating students in a required assignment, midterm, or final examination. The process of testing in step 6, however, is not testing the student but (1) testing and evaluating the designed instruction that has been given to the students in order to learn the required performance objectives and (2) revising the instruction where instructional problems occur for the improvement of student learning.

Evaluation is a process of defining, obtaining, and providing useful information for making decisions that will enhance the teaching/learning process. Evaluation is a process, not an outcome; it follows a sequence of steps and should be continuous throughout the design stage as well as after the course has been implemented. It describes or defines constructive data that can be evaluated and used to make informed decisions for the improvement of the teaching/learning process.

By regularly incorporating evaluation into the design process, developers and online teachers begin to understand the impact of their designed instructional strategies on the teaching/learning process (Dabbagh & Bannan-Ritland, 2005). To accomplish this, you will need to develop an organized, systematic process of evaluation that should include the following:

1. Determine the purpose, desired results, and methods of evaluation.
2. Formatively evaluate the instructional design prior to its introduction online.
3. Revise online materials according to the results of the formative evaluation.
4. After the course had been implemented, conduct a summative evaluation of the individual activities.
5. Make necessary design changes as a result of the evaluation.

The process of evaluation *should not* be conducted when:

- the evaluation would provide trivial information;
- the results of the evaluation will not be used;
- the evaluation cannot yield useful information;
- the evaluation is premature;
- the evaluation process is not well-planned; or
- the evaluation is forced for political reasons.

Conversely, evaluation *should* be conducted when:

- the results will impact the online course;
- there are specified objectives in the evaluation process;
- there are capable evaluators;
- the online projects and course is ready to be evaluated;
- the results would be used; and
- the evaluation will produce useful information for decision making.

DEVELOP A POSITIVE ATTITUDE TOWARD EVALUATION

For some online instructors, the process of course evaluation poses a real threat of exposing inadequacies that could be used as punitive measures for tenure or merit evaluations. It could also be a source of embarrassment. However, a course evaluation should not be conducted with the intent of using the information in an unconstructive manner. The primary purpose of evaluation is (1) to test the instructional design process to improve human learning, (2) to determine the effectiveness of the instructional strategies, and (3) to provide pertinent information to make necessary instructional changes that will create meaningful learning in authentic environments. Therefore, a positive approach to the evaluation process needs to be maintained.

FORMATIVE AND SUMMATIVE EVALUATION DEFINED

The two types of evaluation we will be discussing here are formative and summative evaluation. You will note very quickly that when and how these evaluations are conducted determines the type of evaluation being conducted. The differences between these two types of evaluation are apparent:

- When the cook tastes the soup, that is *formative evaluation*.
- When the guests taste the soup, that is *summative evaluation*.

Formative Evaluation

Formative evaluation in the ASSIST-Me model is the process of evaluating the instructional process *during* the design phase and is conducted throughout its development. This evaluation focuses primarily on determining the strengths and weaknesses of the instruction while the opportunity to improve instruction still exists (Tessmer, 1993, as cited in Dabbagh & Bannan-Ritland, 2005). You will observe in the ASSIST-Me model that for each stage of the design process, there is a two-way arrow leading from the phase being designed to the evaluation phase of the model and then back to the phase being designed. This signifies that all phases of the design process must continually be evaluated and that each step must be evaluated with all other steps being designed. This interevaluation activity is constantly conducted by the designer and/or the faculty member. For example, during step 1 in the analysis stage, the designer evaluates the students in three basic categories: student demographics, specific entry skills, and learning styles. This information is used during step 2 when the performance objectives are being designed.

Summative Evaluation

Summative evaluation in the ASSIST-Me model is the process of evaluating the online course *after* it has been completed. Frequently, however, designers and teaching faculty are convinced that the online course is successful and evaluation at this stage is not necessary (Moore & Kearsley, 1996). Their supporting data include the project and test results and the number of students who successfully complete the course. However, what is not being measured is (1) the effectiveness of the instruction, that is, how well the students are learning what they are supposed to learn; (2) the efficiency or the time it takes to learn the performance objectives; and (3) and the attitude of the students toward the content of the online course, the designed instruction, course requirements, the delivery system, and so on.

When evaluating any online course, we should separate the instructional strategies that were used to design the online course from the technology that delivers the course. Clark (2000, as cited in Dabbagh & Bannan-Ritland, 2005) believes that all delivery systems, for example, Blackboard, WebCT, and the like, are relatively the same and can deliver the designed instruction to the student equally well. The developers should focus their evaluation efforts on the impact of the instructional strategies rather than on the technological features of the delivery system.

CONDUCTING FORMATIVE EVALUATION

Devising a precise formative evaluation process that would be generally inclusive for all online courses is difficult. Each online course is very unique unto itself. The following elements are unique to each individual course:

- Student population
- Course content and complexity
- Performance objectives
- Design strategies and activities to facilitate learning
- Evaluation processes
- Amount of time it takes to make meaningful evaluations for course improvements

Because of the unique nature of each course, a general procedure will be discussed pertaining to conducting formative evaluation ranging from the informal to formal evaluations.

INFORMAL TO FORMAL FORMATIVE EVALUATIONS

The ASSIST-Me model has been designed as a guide for conducting *informal* formative evaluation. When following the design model, the designer or faculty member should carefully interact, step-by-step, with the model and ask him- or herself the appropriate questions and make decisions based upon (1) his or her own training in the subject content; (2) previous teaching experience; (3) student observations, feedback, experiences, and expectations; and (4) established department, school, or national standards. For example, when designing performance objectives for an online lesson, two major steps are used, that is, the data gathered from step 1 and step 2. Within step 2, formative evaluation takes place when the appropriate skill level is selected for the performance objective (knowledge, comprehension, application, analysis, synthesis, or evaluation). The selection process of the performance level may be based on the background of the students, the level deemed appropriate by the instructor, or skill levels set by state or national standards. When completing the standard for the performance objective, that is, the level or criteria used for evaluation, the developer may have his or her own standards of achievement or there may be department, institution, state, or national standards that must be addressed. This sequence would continue through steps 3, 4, and so on, until the instruction for the individual session has been designed.

At the extreme opposite end of the continuum lies the *formal* formative evaluation. This consists of experimental studies having students randomly assigned to control and experimental groups. The experimental instructional strategy is introduced to the experimental group. Test results are compared using an appropriate statistical procedure. These results are generally more conclusive than an informal formative evaluation approach. However, both time and money are required to conduct this type of evaluation.

CONDUCTING SUMMATIVE EVALUATION

The Traditional Approach

At the end of the course, after all of the assignments have been made, graded, and returned, and just before the final exam is given, the instructor requires the students to complete a course evaluation. This type of summative evaluation is a singular event that takes just a few minutes and is intended to evaluate the entire term or semester course.

The survey instruments, generally designed by a department committee, usually contains 20 to 25 items having some type of 5-point scale, with 1 as the lowest rating and 5 as the highest, or a 5-point Lickert scale, with 1 as "strongly disagree," 5 as "strongly agree," and a noncommittal rating of 3, indicating that the student really does not know how to answer the question, is undecided, or prefers not to answer the question. Most of the statements are general in nature and seek information about:

- the structure of the course;
- the value of text;

- instructional materials;
- course requirements;
- the appropriateness of the exams;
- instructor knowledge of the subject content;
- instructor availability for consultations; and
- instructor interest and sensitivity to student problems.

Some forms even ask students to indicate the grade they expect in the class and to assign the instructor a grade for the teaching of the course.

The students are then asked what they liked about the class and what they did not like about the class and improvements that should be made. Here are some positive student examples:

- "I liked the discussions."
- "The demonstrations were well done."
- "I liked the activities."
- "Class presentations."
- "Group presentations."
- "Developing well-written objectives."
- "Learning educational strategies to incorporate in my class."

A sampling of negative student examples includes:

- "The exams."
- "The lectures."
- "The presentation."
- "The book stuff."
- "Covered too much material."

These data obtained from these student surveys at the end of the course do not provide useful information to make informed changes to improve meaningful learning in any authentic learning environment. First, the survey is only a single event lasting a few minutes administered once during a course that lasted from 10 to 16 weeks in length. Second, the statements are extremely general in nature. One survey question may be for multiple events such as assignments, performances, or tests. Third, the students who are completing the evaluation are novice evaluators evaluating a professional. When asked to specify what they liked or disliked about the class, nonsubstantive comments are made that cannot be used to make informed decisions about changing teaching strategies. Fourth, the types of information sought from the students are reactionary statements found in Kirkpatrick's level 1 evaluation (Kirkpatrick, 1998, as cited in Dabbagh & Bannan-Ritland, 2005). This level 1 evaluation, also known as the happiness rating, solicits students' reactions to and perceptions of online instruction. The correlation between the grade the student will earn in the course and the comments made is quite high. If the student liked the subject content, text, assignments, and instructor, and is earning a high grade in the class, the evaluation will be very positive. Conversely, if the student did not like the course content, text, assignments, and instructor, and is earning a low grade or is not passing, the course evaluation will be very negative.

SUMMATIVE EVALUATION AS A PROCESS

As evaluation was defined earlier in this chapter, it is a process of defining, obtaining, and providing useful information to make informed decisions that will enhance the teaching/learning process. Evaluation was also defined as a process that follows a sequence of steps and should be conducted at multiple points throughout the course. Summative evaluation, conducted after course activities have been completed, should have as its goal a clear purpose, desired results, and a specific and developed method of evaluation.

As a goal, the summative evaluation should measure:

- the effectiveness of the instruction, that is, how well the students are learning the performance objectives;
- the efficiency or the time it takes to learn the performance objectives; and
- the attitude of the students toward course content, instruction, course requirements, etc.

Evaluating Individual Segments of the Course

Rather than the "one-shot" assessment technique, which does not yield meaningful information to make substantive changes, a plethora of course activity can be evaluated immediately after it has been conducted

(Dabbagh & Bannan-Ritland, 2005). The following is an example list of course activities or instructional materials that could be evaluated:

- Reading assignments, both textbook and produced by the instructor
- Online discussions concerning the reading assignments and discussion questions
- Rubrics that describe requirements for various assignments
- Assigned writing projects as well as evaluation criteria
- Projects
- Demonstrations
- Skill learning
- Problem solving
- Self-evaluations
- Portfolios
- Projects using the Web
- Tests

The magnitude of evaluation greatly depends upon the amount of time available to (1) design data-gathering instruments, (2) administer the instruments, (3) analyze the data, and (4) implement the changes.

Methods of Data Gathering

Data can be obtained from the students in a variety of ways that can produce useful information to make design changes. Often overlooked is the simple *observation* of student behavior as they interact with the various activities. These behaviors can be noted on a regular basis and instruction adjusted accordingly. Individual *surveys* can be administered upon completion of an activity that has specific student reactions to the activity. This information can be used since it deals with a singular event and is conducted immediately upon completion of the activity. The reaction is still fresh in the minds of the students. For example, a survey for an assignment may look like this using a 5-point Likert scale:

1. The reading assignment prepared me for the assignment.

   1a. If the reading assignment did not prepare you for the assignment, what would be an appropriate reading? Please list.

2. The directions for the assignment were clear.

2a. If the directions were not clear, please indicate where the directions need to be changed.

2b. What changes would you make?

3. The evaluation criteria were appropriate for the assignment.

3a. If the evaluation criteria were not appropriate, please indicate the criteria you would use.

4. The feedback to the assignment was helpful in clarifying mistakes.

4a. If the feedback was not helpful, what would you suggest that would improve the feedback?

For more in-depth data, individual interviews could be conducted. Interviewing the entire class may not be necessary. A set of interview questions should be written in advance. A tape recorder may be helpful in recording student comments. A sampling of students may be sufficient. Focus groups of five or six students could also prove to be rewarding in obtaining data, although it may take slightly longer.

Data Analysis

Once the data has been collected, the next step is to systematically analyze this data. This process sometimes conjures up thoughts of using complicated statistical techniques that are extremely time consuming. Data analysis need not always be complicated, although the need for complex analyses should not be ruled out. At times, a very simple quantitative analysis can produce useful information. The statistical use of central tendency is well within the grasp of instructors. Simple percentages, frequency distributions, and mean scores can produce much-needed information to make design changes. Qualitative analysis of student comments should also be considered, especially when the interview or focus group techniques are used. Comments can be categorized and conclusions may be drawn for design improvements.

Some precautions need to be noted. First, there is a concern that an overabundance of data could be collected. This presents a time-consuming analysis problem. An appropriate sampling technique may need to be employed. Second, the data-gathering instruments need to be very explicit in nature and carefully designed. It may be appropriate to have another online instructor or even a small group of students evaluate an instrument before it is administered. Remember, the data collected is only as good as the designed instrument.

Implement Design Changes

After the data has been analyzed comes the task of making decisions about instructional changes. Remember, these changes are based on the collected data for the improvement of student learning. These changes should be implemented as soon as possible so as to maximize the effect of the improvement. Making instructional design changes at the end of the course is possible if it is not possible to make these changes at any other time. The changes certainly should be made prior to the course the next time it is offered.

A MODEL APPROACH TO SUMMATIVE EVALUATION

The online instructor has done the summative evaluation approach up to this point. This type of self-analysis has some obvious advantages. The online instructor is closest to the content of the course, the instructional materials, the activities, and the students. The online instructor is also a stakeholder in this online course and has time and energy invested to make it successful.

Because the instructor is familiar with his or her course, however, certain limitations may creep into the summative evaluation process. For example, in some cases, the instructor may be extremely certain that the instructional design is the best it can be and therefore, is unwilling to make changes. Also, there may be cases when the instructor is so immersed in the design process that some changes that should be made go unnoticed. In addition, a questionnaire designed by the instructor may be biased and not well constructed or tested. Data obtained from this type of evaluation generally does not yield substantive or beneficial information to use in making informed decisions concerning the design or effectiveness of the distance education course. There is a need to move from student evaluations to expert evaluations using both quantitative and qualitative methodologies that will generate beneficial information to make informed decisions for course changes and improvements (Compora, 2000).

The Stake countenance model (Popham, 1988) or a similar model or process should be used to obtain course data. This evaluation process, if

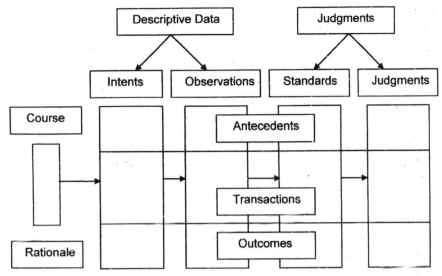

Stake Countenance Model

properly used, will yield specific and beneficial information whereby substantive course changes may be made to ensure that the instructor is teaching what is supposed to be taught and the students are learning what they
are supposed to learn. This evaluation process is divided into five distinct
steps. The first three phases of this process are descriptive, that is, *describing* (1) the course rationale, (2) the intent of the course, and (3) what
was observed. The second phase of the process deals with the evaluator's
judgment by (1) using standards that have been designed by the department, college, or institution, or by using standards established by a professional organization, and then (2) comparing what was observed to
these standards for evaluation. Three other forms of description can be
used as input: antecedents, transactions, and outcomes. Antecedents are
events that have been planned to be included in the course. The transactions are events that occur during the course, and outcomes are the direct
result of the transactions. For example, a demonstration was planned and
given on the use of a microscope. The outcome of this demonstration was
that students were able to properly use the microscope.

THE DESCRIPTIVE DATA PHASE

For the *course rationale* section, the need for the course to be delivered
online must be clearly stated. A review of the course analysis, found in

step 1 of the ASSIST-Me model, is necessary, for example: Is the online course required for a program of study? Are there sufficient numbers of students to support the online course? Are there adequate resources for the course, both academic and technical support? Is there institutional support available for the student, such as access to the library and other student services?

The *intent* section deals with what was planned to be included in the course, or inputs. This includes knowledge objectives, reading assignments, learning activities, demonstrations, projects, and so on.

The *observation* phase is the actual assessment of what was actually included in the course, in other words, there may have been performance objectives included in the syllabus as inputs, but not incorporated in any of the class sessions. Observations should be made at the time class activities occur throughout the course to obtain sufficient information.

THE JUDGMENT PHASE

The *standards*, the fourth phase of this evaluation process in which the course will be compared and judged, can be difficult to establish and select. The standards to be applied to this evaluation process should be appropriate for the course and discipline of study. Standards may be set by the department or institution or may be established by a professional organization within the discipline. Not to be overlooked are the performance objectives written for the course that should also be used as standards to evaluate the effectiveness of the course, in other words, did the students learn what they were supposed to learn?

Finally, a *judgment* will be made by comparing what was intended to be included in the course to what was observed in the course to the standards set for evaluation. The judgment of the evaluator must be unbiased and useful to make informed decisions for course improvement.

THE USE OF AN OUTSIDE EVALUATOR

This evaluation process needs an *evaluator* for the duration of the course. Unlike traditional course evaluations that customarily take place at the end of the course using a single student survey to obtain course data, this type of evaluation should take place several times during the course, as the activities occur, to gather sufficient data to make informed decisions.

A few criteria for the selection of this evaluator need to be established. The evaluator:

- must be familiar with the evaluation process;
- should not be a stakeholder in the course, that is, the evaluator should not be affected by the outcome of the evaluation;
- must be objective in the evaluation process; and
- must have the time and resources to make the judgments.

Remember, this evaluation process is to improve student learning by making specific changes in the design of the course. The intent is neither to embarrass the instructor nor to point out any teaching weaknesses. The intent of this evaluation is to create a learning atmosphere where students may maximize learning in a minimum amount of time.

SUMMARY

Evaluation is a process of defining, obtaining, and providing useful information for making decisions that will enhance the teaching/learning process. Evaluation is a process and not an outcome; it follows a sequence of steps and should be continuous throughout the design stage as well as after the course has been implemented. It describes or defines constructive data that can be evaluated and used to make informed decisions for the improvement of the teaching/learning process. By regularly incorporating evaluation into the design process, developers and online teachers can begin to understand the impact of their designed instructional strategies on the teaching/learning process.

A course evaluation should be conducted with the intent of using the information in a constructive manner. The primary purpose of evaluation is (1) to test the instructional design process to improve human learning, (2) to determine the effectiveness of the instructional strategies, and (3) to provide pertinent information to make necessary instructional changes that will create meaningful learning in authentic environments. Therefore, the need to maintain a positive approach toward the evaluation process is necessary.

Formative evaluation, in the ASSIST-Me model, is the process of evaluating the instructional process *during* the design phase and it is conducted throughout its development. This evaluation focuses primarily on determining the strengths and weaknesses of the instruction while the opportunity to improve instruction still exists.

Summative evaluation, in the ASSIST-Me model, is the process of evaluating the online course *after* it has been completed. What is being measured is (1) the effectiveness of the instruction, that is, how well the students are learning what they are supposed to learn, (2) the efficiency or the time it takes to learn the performance objectives, and (3) the attitude of the student toward the content of the online course, the designed instruction, course requirements, the delivery system, and so on.

The ASSIST-Me model has been designed as a guide for conducting informal formative evaluation. When following the design model the designer or faculty member should be carefully interacting with the model step by step and asking himself the appropriate questions and making decisions based upon (1) his own training in the subject content; (2) previous teaching experience; (3) student observations, feedback, experiences, and expectations; and (4) established department, school, or national standards. At the extreme opposite end of the continuum lies the formal formative evaluation consisting of an experimental design. These results are generally more conclusive than the informal formative evaluation approach. However, both additional time and money are required to conduct this type of evaluation.

Traditional summative evaluation occurs at the end of the course, after all of the assignments have been made, graded, returned, and just before the final exam is given. This type of summative evaluation is a singular event that takes just a few minutes and is intended to evaluate the entire term or semester course. The data obtained from these student surveys at the end of the course does not provide useful information to make informed changes to improve meaningful learning in any authentic learning environment.

As a goal, the summative evaluation should measure:

- the effectiveness of the instruction, that is, how well the students are learning the performance objectives;
- the efficiency or the time it takes to learn the performance objectives; and
- the attitude of the students student toward course content, instruction, course requirements, etc.

Methods of gathering data include observations, surveys, interviews, and focus groups. Data analysis need not always be complicated, although the need for complex analyses should not be ruled out. At times, a very simple quantitative analysis can produce useful information. The statistical use of central tendency is well within the grasp of instructors. Simple percentages, frequency distributions, and mean scores can produce much-needed information to make design changes. Qualitative analysis of student comments should also be considered, especially when the interview or focus group techniques are used. Remember, these changes are based on the collected data for the improvement of student learning. These changes should be implemented as soon as possible so as to maximize the effect of the improvement.

A comprehensive evaluation model or process to obtain course data should be used. This evaluation process, if properly used, will yield specific and beneficial information whereby substantive course changes may be made to insure the course is teaching what it is supposed to teach and the students are learning what they are supposed to learn.

This evaluation process may be divided into five distinct steps. The first three phases of this process are descriptive, that is, *describing* (1) the course rationale, (2) the intent of the course, and (3) what was observed. The second phase of the process deals with the evaluator's *judgment* by (1) using standards that have been designed by the department, college, or institution, or by using standards established by a professional organization, and then (2) comparing what was observed to these standards for evaluation.

This evaluation process needs an outside evaluator for the duration of the course. Unlike traditional course evaluations that customarily take place at the end of the course using a single student survey to obtain course data, this type of evaluation should take place several times during the course to gather sufficient data to make informed decisions.

A few criteria for the selection of this evaluator need to be established, however. The evaluator:

- must be familiar with the evaluation process;
- should not be a stakeholder in the course, that is, the evaluator should not be affected by the outcome of the evaluation;
- must be objective in the evaluation process; and
- must have the time and resources to make the judgments.

CASE STUDIES

Course Description No. 1

Course: BIOL 6000/8000 Introduction to Scientific Thought and Expression
Instructor: Dr. Earnest DuBrul, associate professor, biology

Dr. DuBrul has developed a specific online summative evaluation for his course.

A sincere, in-depth response to each of the following questions will be greatly appreciated. You may attach additional pages if necessary. Also, please feel free to remain anonymous.

1. Comment on the ways this course has helped you learn to be a better interpreter of the issues considered. Did this course help you understand the connections between topics and disciplines? Did you gain in your understanding of critical inquiry? Did this course improve your writing and/or discussion skills?
2. Would you recommend this course to another teacher? Why or why not?
3. How would you describe this seminar to another teacher?
4. Did you invest as much of yourself in this class as you do in your other classes? If not, what would enable you to invest more in this class?
5. What did you like best about this course? What did you like least?
6. Are there materials not covered in this course that you would like to see included?
7. Please comment on the success of the distance learning instruction in this course. What would you suggest to improve the instruction?
8. Please comment on the success of the instructor in this course. What would you suggest for him to improve the instruction?
9. Are there any other topics that you or your colleagues would like to see covered in a DL Biology course?

Course Description No. 2

Course: MET 3100 Applied Thermodynamics
Instructor: Dr. Ella Fridman, associate professor, engineering technology

Students are monitored during the course for problems with completion of module questions and laboratory experiments. Students are encouraged to

(continued)

(continued)

e-mail the instructor and go to a chat room for more in-depth sessions concerning a given question.

Students evaluate the course upon its completion. Evaluation is submitted to both the instructor and the department chairperson for review and revision of course.

Course Description No. 3

Course: CIEC 3200 Philosophy and Practice in Early Childhood Education
Instructor: Dr. Bob Cryan, professor, early childhood education

Formative evaluation is continuous during the time the instruction is developed. The instructor uses the principles and theories developed in the study of early childhood as criteria. After it is posted, the instruction is carefully monitored for student questions and confusion that may occur. Corrections and clarifications to the instruction are made where needed. All students are notified of the modification.

Summative evaluation is made at the end of the course using a specially designed evaluation for online courses.

REFERENCES

Compora, D. (2000). *An investigation of administrative practices and procedures of distance education programs at selected institutions of higher learning in Ohio.* Unpublished Doctoral Dissertation, The University of Toledo, Toledo, OH.

Dabbagh, N., & Bannan-Ritland, B. (2005). *Online learning: concepts, strategies, and application.* Upper Saddle River, NJ: Pearson/Merrill/Prentice Hall.

Jonassen, D., Howland, J., Moore, J., & Marra, R. (2003). *Learning to solve problems with technology: A constructivist perspective* (2nd ed.). Upper Saddle River, NJ: Merrill.

Kirkpatrick, D. L. (1998). *Evaluating training programs: The four levels* (2nd ed.). San Francisco: Barrett-Koehler.

Moore, M., & Kearsley, G. (1996). *Distance education: A systems view.* Belmont, CA: Wadsworth.

Popham, W. (1988). *Educational evaluation.* (2nd ed.). Englewood Cliffs, NJ: Prentice Hall.

CHAPTER 10

Step 7: Maintenance of an Online Course

CHAPTER OUTLINE

The Typical Classroom
   Emphasis on the Individual Student
   Little Meaningful Interaction
Learning Communities
Meaningful Learning Is Cooperative
The Need for Learning Communities
The Purpose of a Learning Community
Strengths and Weaknesses of a Learning Community
   Strengths
   Weaknesses
Research Findings
Building a Learning Community
Communication Among Students and Class
Summary
Case Studies
   Course Description No. 1
   Course Description No. 2
   Course Description No. 3
References

PERFORMANCE OBJECTIVES

At the end of this chapter, you should be able to:

1. Compare and contrast a typical classroom student with student in a learning community.
2. List the strengths and weaknesses of a learning community.
3. Define a learning community.
4. Summarize the research findings concerning learning communities.
5. Explain the steps in developing a learning community.
6. Summarize the various forms of communication that may be used by a learning community.
7. Distinguish between asynchronous and synchronous forms of communication that may be used by both learning communities and the online instructor.

LEXICON

Terms to know:

asynchronous
conversation
discussion
knowledge-based community

learning community
synchronous
threaded discussion

After a memorable two-week stay in London, England, my wife and I decided to take a train to Edinburgh, Scotland, rather than fly. When we arrived at Victoria Station in the typical black taxi, a porter greeted us and took our many pieces of luggage to our awaiting train.

After our luggage was safely aboard the train, the conductor inspected our tickets and gave us a lot of information as to where various facilities could be found on the train as well as what we were going to see during our trip. Since it was near lunchtime, the conductor told us the direction we must take to get to the dining car and that lunch would be served until 2:30 p.m. He also informed us where the train would be making its many stops.

As we left Victoria Station, we began to see the rolling green hills of the countryside, much like we would see in Ohio, Indiana, or Illinois. We occasionally saw a large castle in the distance and pondered its name, when it was built, and who had lived there.

As the conductor was making his many rounds and talking with all of the passengers to be sure they were comfortable and to see if they needed anything, I asked him how fast we were traveling. He apologized that we were only traveling about 140 miles an hour. He admitted it was a bit slow, since the train had a maximum speed in excess of 160 miles per hour. The train speed had to be reduced due to the slowness of the electronic switching system ahead of us. He assured us, however, that it still would only take us four hours to travel to Edinburgh, even with all of the stops.

An online course is much like taking a high-speed train ride to a given destination. The online course is the train that takes the passengers, or students, to a given destination of learning new knowledge, skills, and attitudes. The conductor on the train is the instructor, who supervises the passenger-student during the time it takes to arrive at the final destination.

Once the online course has been implemented, the instructional design of the course needs to be maintained. As a train needs regular checkups and maintenance to prevent breakdowns and expensive repairs, an online course also needs regular checkups and maintenance to prevent learning breakdowns and instructional repairs. Conducting the online course does not stop when the course is implemented. The maintenance is continuous by the conductor-instructor to assist the students along the way when they are in need of information, direction, and consultation.

THE TYPICAL CLASSROOM

Emphasis on the Individual Student

The typical classroom is composed of individual learners who are passive and complete assignments when directed by the instructor. Course content is generally textbook centered, with a set of performance objectives and course activities that will reinforce the performance objectives. Learning course content and required skills is an independent responsibility. Resources are generally restricted to the classroom or Internet. Summative evaluation is dependent upon individual performance and focuses on grades.

Little Meaningful Interaction

There is little social interaction with other students during the class. When discussions do occur, student contributions are generally superficial and opinions are offered with no supporting evidence. For the most part, discussions are customarily nondirective and occur sporadically, only when questions are raised by either the instructor or students.

Frequently, what is thought to be a class discussion concerning a specific topic becomes a more general conversation. There is a distinct difference between a conversation and an authentic discussion. Conversations occur on a regular basis and do not have an agenda. They are nondirective and topics regularly change based upon individual preferences of topics. When a conversation ends, only superficial information has been exchanged with no change in knowledge, skills, or attitudes.

Authentic class discussions, however, are very specific and focus on a precise topic or question that has multiple subtopics that need to be addressed. Statements made by individual students demonstrate critical-thinking skills by making specific references to related literature, relating course content to prior knowledge, and interpreting content through analysis, synthesis, and evaluation of others' understanding (Dabbagh & Bannan-Ritland, 2005). A discussion leader, whose responsibility is to keep the group attentive to the topic, guides the contributions made by the group through the subtopics. The discussion leader also clarifies comments made and keeps the groups working together as a cohesive unit. Individual contributions are based on learners' knowledge and are normally supported by research, the literature in the field, and noted authorities. The discussion leader will, when it is appropriate, summarize the contributions or have one of the discussants summarize the contributions before moving on to the next agenda item. When meaningful discussion has been concluded, a summation is made that offers to solve the question or problem. The result of this discussion should be meaningful learning of knowledge, skills, and attitudes.

LEARNING COMMUNITIES

The learning community stands in stark contrast to the typical classroom atmosphere of the independent student. Individuals belong to various types of communities, each having its own purpose, interest, and activity (Jonassen et al., 2003). These communities can comprise work-related activities, such as a department in a business or a legal firm, or religious, social, fraternal, or neighborhood activities. A community can also be thought of as a group of students who are all enrolled in the same course. The purpose, interest, and activity in this community focus more on learning and knowledge and where information may be located. This community could also be more specifically referred to as a knowledge-based or learning community.

In a knowledge-based community, the students construct their knowledge with a focus on the process as well as the product (Buffington, 2003). The learning that takes place is social in nature, but with an emphasis on fostering inquiry and problem solving. The curriculum contains authentic problems from real-life situations. Information is accessed from multiple authoritative sources. Evaluation includes formative assessment and focus on self-improvement. Reflection is an integral part of the process.

MEANINGFUL LEARNING IS COOPERATIVE

Moreover, it is common to observe students outside of class seeking others to help them solve various course issues with the readings, class assignments, impending tests, and so on. These informal student gatherings have several names. Some refer to them as hallway sessions, dorm room sessions, or even "bull" sessions. This type of learning session often helps students to a better understanding and aids their success in the course.

This author has observed, over many years of teaching, that when groups of four to six students were assigned to solve a problem of the use of technology for a teaching/learning situation, the response to this type of activity was extremely positive. The community of students, when given an opportunity to use text material, Internet information, and group knowledge and teaching experience, had an extremely positive attitude and indicated they learned from others within their group. When the course was completed and the traditional course evaluation was administered, the majority of students indicated that the best elements of the course were the group projects and the reporting of their findings. The students also indicated that they learned a lot from the other groups when they gave their reports.

THE NEED FOR LEARNING COMMUNITIES

Distance education has been defined as the delivery of an organized body of knowledge using some form of technology to bridge the geographical separation of the instructor from the student. Notice in the definition it is the instructor who is separated from the student. Separation also occurs with the student. The student is separated not only from the instructor, but also separated from the other students in the online class. There is no sense of the traditional classroom where a student can see and hear other students' questions and comments or lean toward another student and quietly whisper a question and receive an answer.

A graduate student made the following comments when evaluating a distance education course.

> There was a lack of social interaction with classmates and instructors. Spontaneity of discussion was lost. The sense of connection that a person gets by being involved with a live class is lost. You tend to see oneself as a class of one and no others.

The need for students to interact with one another and to establish a community is important and is illustrated in the following example about nature.

The Sense of a Goose
Author Unknown

Next autumn, when you see geese heading south for the winter, flying in a long "V" formation, you might consider what science has discovered about why they fly that way.

As each bird flaps its wings, it creates uplift for the bird immediately following. By flying in a "V" formation, the whole flock adds at least 71% more flying range than possible if each bird flew on its own.

People who share common direction and sense of community can get where they are going more quickly and easily because they are traveling on the thrust of one another.

When a goose falls out of formation, it suddenly feels the drag and resistance of trying to do it alone and quickly gets back into formation to take advantage of the lifting power of the bird in front.

If we have as much sense as a goose, we will stay in formation with those who are headed the same way.

When the head goose gets tired, it rotates back in the wing and another goose takes the lead.

It is sensible to take turns doing demanding jobs, whether with people or with geese flying south.

Geese honk from behind to encourage those up front to keep up their speed.

What do we say when we hear a honk from behind?

Finally, and this is important, when a goose gets sick or wounded by gunshot and falls out of formation, two other geese fall out with that goose and follow it down to lend help and protection. They stay with the fallen goose until it is able to fly or until it dies. Only then do they launch out on their own or with another formation to catch up with the group.

If we have the sense of a goose, we will stand by each other that way!

THE PURPOSE OF A LEARNING COMMUNITY

As we have learned from geese flying in a *V* formation, the purpose of a learning community is to learn together and from one another (Jonassen et al., 2003). A learning community is a social organization of people who have varied abilities, strengths, and skills and who share knowledge, values, and goals. A learning community emerges when learners work together toward their common goal. Rather than always forcing students to conform to a prepackaged set of instructional learning goal requirements, designers should also consider the contributions that can be made by a group of learners toward the same learning goal.

STRENGTHS AND WEAKNESSES OF A LEARNING COMMUNITY

As with any form of teaching/learning methodology, both the strengths and weaknesses must be carefully weighed and evaluated before they are used. The online instructor has the responsibility to make a decision as to the amount of involvement the learning community will have within the course.

Strengths

- Students collaborate or co-labor to solve the given problem. Strength is found in working together as a team to reach the goal.
- Individual knowledge, skills, and strengths are shared among the community.
- Group contributions tend to be better in knowledge building to solve the objective.
- Social skills of communication and negotiation are practiced and improved.
- Solving the problem becomes learning a process.
- The solution to the problem tends to be more accurate.

Weaknesses

- The community may have to be trained in working together.
- There may be incompatible members in the community.
- More time is needed to solve the problem.
- Individuals in the community can sway others to accept an incorrect solution to the problem.
- Not all community members may make an appropriate amount of contribution.
- The community must rely on individual strengths, skills, and knowledge.
- The community may lack the ability to properly evaluate a solution to the problem.

RESEARCH FINDINGS

Research in the employment of learning communities is sparse. Researchers tend to be more concerned with the interaction of the student with the online lecture, a lecture with televised video inserts, a tele-lecture, audio, and so on, rather than with students interacting with each other (Beare, 1989, cited in Simonson et al., 2003). Researchers are still concentrating on the individual student interacting with various forms of instructional formats and neglecting the value found in students working as a learning community. Conclusions drawn from this type of research study tend to conclude that individual instructional formats or amount of interaction have little effect on student achievement. However, this could be a result of the conditioned passive response of individual students.

Another study found that distance education students tended to bond more with fellow classmates and the instructor (Souder, 1993, cited in Simonson et al., 2003). They appeared supportive of each other and thought they performed better than traditional classroom groups. They gained a valuable network of colleagues and skills by working together in a collaborative manner.

No final or definitive conclusions may be drawn from previous research. Simonson et al. (2003) summarized their research findings on distance education by stating: "Focusing on building collaboration and group interaction may be more important than focusing on individual participation." From this conclusion, it is encouraging that researchers are beginning to recognize the possible worth of learning communities and their contribution and the need to conduct research in this area.

BUILDING A LEARNING COMMUNITY

Naturally, students converse with one another. In a traditional course, students interact with each other as soon as they enter the classroom for the first time and continue until the instructor formally begins the class. Some instructors, before they even begin discussing their syllabus, have the students complete a student information sheet. This sheet contains basic information about the student such as name, major and minor, telephone number, and e-mail address. Next, there may be some basic questions such as what the students want to learn in the class, their educational goals, previous experience they have had in this area of study, and possibly their interests and hobbies. Upon completion, the students introduce themselves to the class and share this information.

Students enrolled in an online course have the same social needs as students enrolled in a traditional classroom. They want to know the other students and become acquainted. However, because of the separation of the instructor and the students and the student from the other students, it is necessary that you create an opportunity for the students to get acquainted.

The following is a suggested procedure for students to gradually get acquainted and begin to work together as a learning community.

1. *Have students post their biography.* As the student information sheet is completed in the classroom, the online students can be asked for much the same information. However, you may want to ask students to include specific information about their academic major and the type of profession they intend to pursue upon graduation. In addition,

you may want them to address their academic experiences and skills they possess as well as job experiences. Then have the students post their biographies in a discussion forum and require all of the students to read each other's biographies.

2. *Group students to answer a meaningful question.* Next, group the students into pairs or small groups of three to four students. This may be done either by student self-selection or by the instructor based on student skill backgrounds. Then assign all groups the same question to answer. Give the groups a deadline to post their answer. Assign specific groups to critique the answer of another group and post their critique. Using the same discussion forum format, the instructor should then summarize the critiques in a live chat room.

3. *Regroup students to analyze a case study.* The third activity is to have students further get acquainted by having students grouped who have not previously worked together. Students can select their own groups, or the instructor may assign the small groups. Each group should be given a different case study to examine. Set a deadline for when the analysis must be posted in the discussion forum. Once all cases studies have been posted, assign groups to critique each other's case studies and post their critiques on the discussion forum. Using the same discussion forum, the instructor should have the groups summarize what was learned in the process.

COMMUNICATION AMONG STUDENTS AND CLASS

Before you assign groups to work together to answer a meaningful question or to analyze a case study, it is necessary to explain the various options of communication that are available. When low-tech communication is possible, it is not always necessary to employ high-tech forms of communication.

1. *Live meetings.* If it is possible, and if geographical location and time permits, students may be encouraged to get together at a common location to work on their question or case study. More can be done in a shorter period of time when there is a face-to-face meeting for a rapid exchange of ideas.

2. *Cell phones.* Practically all students either have a cell phone or can gain easy access to a cell phone on which conference calls may be

made. In this case, no geographical boundary is present. Students may set a designated time for their discussions.

3. *E-mail.* This type of communication, which is a slightly higher form of technology, should be very common to all students. If they do not yet have an e-mail account, they should be encouraged to get one as soon as possible for your course. Web-based e-mail accounts are available at no cost from several sources or from your own institution (Kearsley, 2000). The main advantage of the use of e-mail is the ability to send quick evaluative comments to members of the group as well as to provide attachments containing detailed analysis of the question or case study. Members of the group may then study these attachments. Individual members can then e-mail feedback statements to the attachments to the entire group. Obviously, e-mail may be used quite effectively for small groups as well as for the entire class.

4. *Threaded discussions.* The next most common communication device for an online course is the threaded discussion system of conferencing, a forum, or bulletin board. As with e-mail, this is also an asynchronous system of communication. Although these systems vary, they work in a similar fashion (Kearsley. 2000). Topics and subtopics are created and students post messages under various topics or subtopics. These messages include the sender's name, subject title, and text of the message.

   For all students enrolled in the online course, a conference system may be created in several different ways (Kearsley, 2000). New topics can be created by any member of the class or only by the instructor. Only the topics are displayed with hidden subtopics or, if desired, both topics and subtopics may be displayed. Messages are posted directly or may be previewed by you before being posted. Some systems identify new messages or unread messages and some allow messages to be classified as agreements, disagreements, or rebuttals.

   The use of a discussion board within the online course permits you as the instructor to post questions or problems that correspond to a topic of discussion in the class. Students can then post their responses as subtopics. This discussion may be conducted over a few days or a week. All class members can read the responses posted by other class members.

5. *Synchronous conferencing.* After the students have posted the results of the questions or case studies, you may conduct a live conversation

using a chat session. All of the students see the comments as soon as they are sent. Each message contains the name of the sender.

This type of chat room can also be established for the learning groups. Each group can be assigned a specific time to conduct live chats to work on their respective question or case study.

SUMMARY

The typical classroom is composed of individual learners who are passive and complete assignments when directed by the instructor. Course content is generally textbook centered, with a set of performance objectives and course activities that will reinforce the performance objectives. Learning course content and required skills is an independent responsibility. Resources are generally restricted to the classroom or Internet. Summative evaluation is dependent upon individual performance and focuses on grades. There is little social interaction with other students during the class. When discussions do occur, student contributions are generally superficial and opinions are offered with no supporting evidence. For the most part, discussions are customarily nondirective and sporadically occur only when questions are raised by either the instructor or students.

Frequently, what is thought to be a class discussion concerning a specific topic becomes a more general conversation. Conversations occur on a regular basis and do not have an agenda. They are nondirective and topics regularly change based upon individual preferences of topics. When a conversation ends, only superficial information has been exchanged, with no change in knowledge, skills, or attitudes.

Authentic class discussions, however, are very specific and focus on a precise topic or question that has multiple subtopics that need to be addressed. Statements made by individual students demonstrate critical thinking skills by making specific references to related literature, relating course content to prior knowledge, and interpreting content through analysis, synthesis, and evaluation of others' understanding. The result of this discussion should be meaningful learning of knowledge, skills, and attitudes.

In contrast to the typical classroom atmosphere of the independent student is the learning community. Communities can be thought of as a group of students who are all enrolled in the same course. The purpose, interest, and activity in this community focuses more on learning and knowledge and how it is acquired. Students construct their knowledge with a focus on the process and the product. The curriculum contains authentic problems from real-life situations. Information is accessed from multiple authoritative sources. Evaluation includes formative assessment and focus on self-improvement. Reflection is an integral part to the process.

The following is a suggested procedure for students to gradually get acquainted and begin to work together as a learning community.

1. Have students post their biographies.
2. Group students to answer a meaningful question.
3. Regroup students to analyze a case study.

CASE STUDIES

Course Description No. 1

Course: BIOL 6000/8000 Introduction to Scientific Thought and Expression
Instructor: Dr. Earnest DuBrul, associate professor, biology

Each student is required, on a weekly basis, to post responses and feedback to a list of questions contained in the individual sessions. Group discussions using the chat rooms are conducted regularly.

Course Description No. 2

Course: MET 3100 Applied Thermodynamics
Instructor: Dr. Ella Fridman, associate professor, engineering technology

Students are encouraged to e-mail student partners and the instructor for direction and additional material.

Course Description No. 3

Course: CIEC 3200 Philosophy and Practice in Early Childhood Education
Instructor: Dr. Bob Cryan, professor, early childhood education

Students are required to be engaged in this course in small group activities for selected chapters as well as to attend weekly live chats. There are two 45-minute live chat discussions. Each student is required to attend at least one of these live chats. Students may also elect to attend both chat sessions. During these live chats, questions about the current chapter are discussed and linked to threaded discussion questions. The instructor monitors student responses. If students do not become engaged, the instructor will send a private message to those students to get involved in the chat session.

REFERENCES

Buffington, J. (2003). Learning communities as an instructional model. Retrieved December 12, 2004, from http://coe.uga.edu/eplitt/lc.htm.

Dabbagh, N., & Bannan-Ritland, B. (2005). *Online learning concepts, strategies and application*. Columbus: Merrill Prentice Hall.

Jonassen, D., Howland, J., Moore, J., & Marra, R. (2003). *Learning to solve problems with technology: A constructivist perspective*. (2nd ed.). Upper Saddle River, NJ: Merrill.

Kearsley, G. (2000). *Online education: Learning and teaching in cyberspace*. Stamford, CT: Wadsworth Thomson Learning.

Simonson, M., Smaldino, S., Albright, M., & Zvacek, S. (2003). *Teaching and learning at a distance: Foundations of distance education*. (2nd ed.). Upper Saddle River, NJ: Merrill/Prentice Hall.

Appendix

STEP 1: ANALYZE STUDENTS (CHAPTER 4)

1. Student demographics: level of education, age, gender, ethnicity, socioeconomic background. Age and gender are not necessarily important for college students.

   - Generally, undergraduate students have fairly well-developed learning skills and have elected to pursue a bachelor's degree; need to observe the years of schooling obtained, for example, freshman, sophomore, junior, or senior.
   - Graduate students have elected to further their career goals and have much better-developed learning skills; graduate students study to learn course content.
   - Number of students is important for class management.
   - Socioeconomic background may be relatively unimportant for undergraduate or graduate students.

2. Specific entry-level skills

   2.1. Identify skills the students possess regarding general required courses in major field and required prerequisite skills, if they apply.
   2.2. Identify specific skills students need for this course.

3. Learning styles

   3.1. *Concrete sequential*: Students prefer enactive learning that is structured in a logical order using a hands-on approach, as in using a workbook, drill-and-practice, and student demonstrations.
   3.2. *Concrete random*: Students learn best in an atmosphere of trial-and-error learning. Students prefer games, simulations, independent learning, and discovery learning.

3.3. *Abstract sequential*: Students decode information from reading and processing classroom lecture/discussions.

3.4. *Abstract random*: Students learn from mediated instruction, for example, PowerPoint or videos.

Note: Generally, about 80 to 85% of students are visual learners and 15 to 20% are verbal learners.

STEP 2: STATE PERFORMANCE OBJECTIVES USING THE 4S METHOD (CHAPTER 5)

1. Student: The student who will be taking the course, for example, the engineering student, the biology student, the early childhood student.
2. Skill: The new performance behavior to be learned. Skill must be observable and measurable. Must eliminate performances that are vague, such as to know, to understand, to appreciate, or to enjoy.
3. Supplies: What the student will be given in order to complete the objective, for example, a calculator in an engineering class, a microscope in biology, or a taxonomy of adolescent behaviors for an early childhood class.
4. Standards: The level at which the student will be evaluated. *Qualitative* criteria will deal with how well the student performed, for example, 70%, 80%, 90%, or 100% levels. *Quantitative* criteria will deal with how much students have been able to accomplish, for example, demonstrated three pieces of technology in nine minutes.

STEP 3: SELECT INSTRUCTIONAL CONTENT, ORGANIZATION OF CONTENT, AND MEDIA (CHAPTER 6)

Instructional content: Consult references at the end of textbook chapter. Search for additional support using appropriate search methods on the Web. Use key descriptors.

Select appropriate support material: Obtain material that will reinforce lesson content such as illustrations, examples, hypothetical situations, quotations, comparisons, and humor.

Order instructional content: *Chronological* order refers to dates; *sequential* order refers to a step-by-step process; *topical* order is organizing material in the most interesting manner.

Design summary: Summary serves as a review of lesson content. Can summarize performance objectives. Summary may be a miniature chapter review of main points.

STEP 4: IMPLEMENT INSTRUCTION (CHAPTER 7)

Design extended syllabus—see chapter 7.

Design individual sessions into modules—a self-contained unit of instruction.

Module design procedures using a template found in chapter 7.

STEP 5: SOLICIT STUDENTS' RESPONSES TO INSTRUCTION (CHAPTER 8)

Engage students in authentic tasks, in meaningful ways, and in a problem-solving approach.

An authentic problem is a problem that is clearly stated, generally has only one way to solve the problem, and has a single answer.

An ill-defined problem is not clearly defined and has multiple ways to achieve the solution, that is, has no single answer.

STEP 6: TEST, EVALUATE, AND REVISE INSTRUCTION (CHAPTER 9)

Evaluation of instruction design is the process of defining, obtaining, and providing useful information for making decisions that will enhance the teaching/learning process:

- Determine the purpose of evaluation, including desired results;
- Formally evaluate the instructional design prior to its introduction online;
- Revise online instruction according to the results of the formative evaluation.

Types:

Formative evaluation in the ASSIST-Me model is the process of evaluating the instruction during the design phase, and it is conducted throughout its development.

Summative evaluation in the ASSIST-Me model is the process of evaluating the online course after it has been completed.

STEP 7: MAINTENANCE OF AN ONLINE COURSE (CHAPTER 10)

Building a learning community is to learn together and from one another. A learning community emerges when learners work together toward a common goal.

When forming a learning community: 1) have students post their biography; 2) group students to answer a meaningful question; and 3) regroup students to analyze a case study.

About the Authors

Franklin R. Koontz began his career in distance education as an instructional television producer/director for the University Division of Instructional Services at the Pennsylvania State University in 1966. For two years he produced and directed distance education courses for the main campus as well as for 19 branch campuses. In 1968, he became the first instructional television producer/director for University Television Services at the University of Toledo. During his professional career as an ITV producer/director, he managed to produce and direct more than 5,000 distance education productions. Culminating his career as the director of University Television Services, Dr. Koontz began to teach educational technology courses on a full-time basis in 1985 for the College of Education. During his tenure as a professor of educational technology, he wrote several articles, gave multiple national presentations, and wrote a textbook, *Media and Technology in the Classroom*. He conducted several research studies in distance education and workshops in designing instruction for Web-based courses, as well as directed several doctoral dissertations regarding teaching and learning at a distance. His real passion is teaching principles of distance teaching and learning and the administration of distance education programs.

Hongqin Li earned her Ph.D. in educational technology from the University of Toledo. She taught at the University of Toledo as a visiting professor of educational technology for two years and is currently an assistant professor of instructional technology at Lourdes College, Sylvania, Ohio, where she teaches instructional design, Web-based instruction, multimedia for educators, and other technology courses.

As a member of the International Society for Technology in Education (ISTE) and the Association for Educational Communications and Technology (AECT), Dr. Li has strong connections to the ever-changing field of technology. She has presented papers at international conferences in the field of instructional technology. Prior to her doctoral study in educational technology, Dr. Li also taught English as a Second Language in China. She has a total of over ten years teaching experience in higher education.

Daniel P. Compora is an assistant professor of English at the University of Toledo. His content areas of specialty include science fiction and fantasy literature, folklore, and composition. Dr. Compora also serves as a departmental director of computing and teaches all of his courses partially online. He published the article "Computers and Writing: Using Technology to Improve Student Writing" in a regional journal in 1998 and completed his doctoral studies in educational technology at the University of Toledo in 2000. His article "Current Trends in Distance Education: An Administrative Model" was published in the *Online Journal of Distance Learning Administration* in 2003. In addition to his research in the field of distance learning, Dr. Compora has presented in the field of folklore and urban legends.